P9-CBK-340

Modern Critical Interpretations

Modern Critical Interpretations

Tennessee Williams's
Cat on a Hot Tin Roof

Edited and with an introduction by
Harold Bloom
Sterling Professor of the Humanities
Yale University

CHELSEA HOUSE PUBLISHERS
Philadelphia

Printed and bound in the United States of America

10 9 8 7 6 5 4 3 2 1

∞ The paper used in this publication meets the minimum
requirements of the American National Standard for
Permanence of Paper for Printed Library Materials,
Z39.48-1984

Library of Congress Cataloging-in-Publication Data
Tennessee Williams's Cat on a hot tin roof / edited and
    with an introduction by Harold Bloom.
        p. cm.— (Modern critical interpretations)
    Includes bibliographical references and index.
    ISBN 0-7910-6342-9 (alk. paper)
    1. Williams, Tennessee, 1911–1983. Cat on a hot tin roof.
    I. Title: Cat on a hot tin roof.   II. Bloom, Harold.
    III. Series.

    PS3545.I5365 C3734 2001
    812'.54—dc21   2001047400

Chelsea House Publishers
1974 Sproul Road, Suite 400
Broomall, PA 19008-0914

The Chelsea House World Wide Web address is
http://www.chelseahouse.com

Series Editor: Matt Uhler

Contributing Editor: Pamela Loos

Produced by Publisher's Services, Santa Barbara, California

Contents

Editor's Note

My Introduction meditates upon the relative eminence of *Cat* among Williams's major plays.

Brick Pollitt's nihilistic despair is related by Charles E. May to the Keatsian dilemma of identifying truth with beauty, while Roger Boxill, in an overview of *Cat on a Hot Tin Roof*, sensibly indicates Brick's likeness to Big Daddy, both out of place in modern corporate America.

In John M. Clum's view, Brick's homophobia evades realization of his father's homosexual phase, after which David Savran also centers upon the play's partial evasions of full homosexual revelation.

The influence of Federico Garcia Lorca's *Yerma* upon Williams's play is demonstrated by Christopher Brian Weimer, while Susan Koprince discusses Skipper as one of Williams's "unseen characters," akin to Allan Grey in *Streetcar.*

Mark Royden Winchell considers the Brick-Skipper romance in the context of American literature's myth of male companionship, after which Marian Price discusses the changes in the two versions of Act III of the play.

Alice Griffin, commending *Cat*, sees it as near classical tragedy, centering upon a family group, while George W. Crandell concludes this volume by analyzing Brick as a version of the myth of Narcissus.

Introduction

I t is difficult to argue for the aesthetic achievement of Tennessee Williams's long, final phase as a dramatist. Rereading persuades me that his major plays remain *The Glass Menagerie, A Streetcar Named Desire, Suddenly Last Summer,* and the somewhat undervalued *Summer and Smoke. Cat on a Hot Tin Roof* was a popular and critical success, on stage and as a film. I have just reread it in the definitive Library of America edition, which prints both versions of Act III, the original, which Williams greatly preferred, and the Broadway revision, made to accommodate the director Elia Kazan. Here is the ambiguous original conclusion, followed by the revision:

MARGARET: And so tonight we're going to make the lie true, and when that's done, I'll bring the liquor back here and we'll get drunk together, here, tonight, in this place that death has come into . . .
—What do you say?

BRICK: I don't say anything. I guess there's nothing to say.

MARGARET: Oh, you weak people, you weak, beautiful people!— who give up.—What you want is someone to—
(*She turns out the rose-silk lamp.*)
—take hold of you.—Gently, gently, with love! And—
(*The curtain begins to fall slowly.*)
I *do* love you, Brick, I *do!*

BRICK: (*smiling with charming sadness*): Wouldn't it be funny if that was true?

***

1

MARGARET: And you lost your driver's license! I'd phone ahead and
             have you stopped on the highway before you got
             halfway to Ruby Lightfoot's gin mill. I told a lie to Big
             Daddy, but we can make that lie come true. And then
             I'll bring you liquor, and we'll get drunk together,
             here, tonight, in this place that death has come into!
             What do you say? What do you say, baby?

BRICK: (*X to L side bed*)
             I admire you, Maggie.
             (*Brick sits on edge of bed. He looks up at the overhead light,
             then at Margaret. She reaches for the light, turns it out;
             then she kneels quickly beside Brick at foot of bed.*)

MARGARET: Oh, you weak, beautiful people who give up with such
             grace. What you need is someone to take hold of
             you—gently, with love, and hand your life back to you,
             like something gold you let go of—and I can! I'm
             determined to do it—and nothing's more determined
             than a cat on a tin roof—is there? Is there, baby?
             (*She touches his cheek, gently.*)

As Williams noted, his Maggie augments in charm between the two
versions; his Brick modulates subtly, and is a touch more receptive to her.
Shakespeare demonstrates how difficult it is to resist vitality in a stage role,
by creating Sir John Falstaff with a vivacity and wit that carries all before
him. There is nothing Shakespearean about Williams: he sketches arche-
types, caricatures, grotesques, and cannot represent inwardness. And yet,
with all his limitations, he writes well, unlike Eugene O'Neill, who is leaden,
and Arthur Miller, who is drab. Thornton Wilder, Edward Albee, and Tony
Kushner also have their eloquences, but Williams remains the most articulate and adequate of American dramatists up to this moment.

Yet his inability to dramatize inwardness is a considerable limitation.
What is Brick's spiritual malady? His homoeroticism is palpably less a burden
than is his homophobia: he will not accept Big Daddy's earlier bisexuality,
anymore than he could yield to love for Skipper (or to Maggie). Brick's
narcissism is central to the play, but even more crucial would be his nihilism,
if only Williams could tell us something about it. As a Hamlet, Brick does
not work at all; he hasn't enough mind to express what most deeply torments
him, and I fear that Williams shares this lack. What deprives *Cat on a Hot Tin
Roof* of any authentic aesthetic eminence is its obscurantism, which may be
indeliberate, unlike Joseph Conrad's in *Heart of Darkness*. It is as though both
Williams and Brick were saying: "The horror! The horror!" without ever
quite knowing what they were trying to talk about.

The ultimately benign and loving Big Daddy and the adoring Big Mama are *not* the cause of Brick's despair. Were it not for his nihilistic malaise, it seems likely that Brick eventually would turn into his dying father, and would become pragmatically bisexual or pansexual. Brick's attachment to Maggie is ambivalent, but so was his affection for Skipper. As a pure narcissist, Brick is autoerotic, in the manner of Walt Whitman.

The play's epigraph, from Dylan Thomas's "Do not go Gentle into that Good Night," is a gesture of tribute to Big Daddy, who, with Maggie the Cat, saves the play. Brick, without them, would freeze the audience, particularly now, when homosexuality is no longer an issue for an audience not dominated by Fundamentalists, Reagan Republicans, and assorted other mossbacks. Read side-by-side with the wistful *Summer and Smoke*, *Cat on a Hot Tin Roof* seems more a film script than an achieved drama.

CHARLES E. MAY

Brick Pollitt as Homo Ludens: "Three Players of a Summer Game" and Cat on a Hot Tin Roof

If Maggie the Cat is one of Tennessee Williams' most dramatically engaging characters, her husband, Brick Pollitt, is one of his most metaphysically mysterious. Brick's enigmatic detachment in *Cat on a Hot Tin Roof* has been the subject of more problematical commentary than either Maggie's feline restlessness or the spirit of mendacity that dominates the thematic action of the play itself. With his cool ironic smile and relative immobility (suggested both by his literal crutch and by the crutchlike liquor cabinet from which he never strays very far), Brick is, by contrast, the ambiguous center for all the characters in *Cat* who dance about on the hot tin roof of their "common crisis." Because Brick's detachment is thus so crucial, and also because Williams makes him so teasingly mysterious, the central question of the play that has always puzzled critics, a question still unanswered, is: What, apart from its function as catalyst for the dramatic action, does Brick's detachment mean?

In his "Note of Explanation" in the published version of *Cat*, Williams makes it quite explicit that for him Brick's "moral paralysis" is central to the play, a "root thing" in Brick's "tragedy." In fact, Williams felt Brick's problem was so basic to his own conception of *Cat* that of the three changes Elia Kazan urged him to make in the Broadway version of the play, the alteration in Brick's character in the third act is the change to which he devotes most of

From *Tennessee Williams: 13 Essays*, Jac Tharpe, ed. ©1980 by the University Press of Mississippi.

his explanation. Williams complains that such a dramatic progression tends to obscure the meaning of Brick's tragedy, for no matter how revelatory the conversion, it never effects such an immediate change in the "heart or even conduct of a person in Brick's state of spiritual disrepair." Indeed, Nancy Tischler says that as a result of the change in Brick in the third act of the Broadway version, audiences may leave the theater suspecting that the "whole truth" about him has not been told.

However, even those critics who consult Williams' original third act, included in the published version of the play, complain that the meaning of Brick's tragedy remains obscure. Williams' own commentary offers no clarification. He is well aware of the mystery of Brick's personality, and he wishes to leave it that way. "Some mystery should be left in the revelation of character in a play, just as a great deal of mystery is always left in the revelation of character in life, even in one's own character to himself." Although everyone familiar with the play is aware that Brick's disgust with life and resultant detachment has something to do with his homosexual relationship, latent or otherwise, with his friend Skipper, most readers sense that this is not the whole truth. Again, Williams encourages rather than clarifies the ambiguity. As Brick and Big Daddy "timidly and painfully" try to discuss the "inadmissible thing that Skipper died to disavow," Williams comments that the "fact that if it existed it had to be disavowed to 'keep face' in the world they lived in, may be at the heart of the 'mendacity' that Brick drinks to kill his disgust with. It may be the root of his collapse. Or maybe it is only a single manifestation of it, not even the most important."

Throughout the published version of *Cat*, Williams' comments suggest that Brick's problem is spiritual or metaphysical in nature, not simply psychological, and therefore not so liable to "pat" conclusions or "facile definitions which make a play just a play, not a snare for the truth of human experience." What Williams says he wishes to capture in the play is not the solution of one man's psychological problem, but rather the "true quality of experience," the "interplay of live human beings in the thundercloud of a common crisis." However, since much of this "common crisis" is the result of Brick's disgust and detachment, many critics have argued that Brick himself should be more adequately explained. As Benjamin Nelson says, "A true quality of experience cannot be grasped when the situation and characters involved are left unexplained." Signi Lenea Falk even goes so far as to suggest that "Williams writes as if he himself did not know the physical and moral condition of his hero and the reason for his collapse."

Nelson, Falk, and other critics who have accused Williams of obscurantism in regard to Brick have done so precisely because they do not see that Brick's problem is not simply psychological and therefore not solvable by "facile definitions." What is wrong with Brick is rather metaphysical in nature and thus not "knowable" or "explainable," at least not in the way that Nelson and Falk expect when they use those terms. Brick's mysterious disgust can perhaps best be approached by comparing it to the problem of a similar disgust in *Hamlet* as it is analyzed by T. S. Eliot. As Eliot says, although Hamlet's disgust may be occasioned by his mother, she is not an adequate "objective correlative" for it. Similarly, Brick's disgust exceeds the so-called homosexual problem with Skipper. As a result, he, like Hamlet, is unable to understand the cause of his dilemma. In one of the stage directions in act two, when Brick tries to explain himself to a skeptical Big Daddy, Williams describes Brick as a "broken, 'tragically elegant' figure telling simply as much as he knows of 'the Truth'."

The "true quality of experience . . . , that cloudy, flickering, evanescent—fiercely charged!—interplay" that Williams wants to catch in *Cat on a Hot Tin Roof*, does not stem from a psychosexual problem, but rather from the metaphysical implications of some "inadmissible thing" that Williams attempts to objectify by means of Brick's "homosexuality." If the objectification is inadequate, it is not because Williams does not know what the problem is but because it is simply not knowable or explainable in psychological or sexual terms. However, since the psychosexual answer is such an easy if not completely satisfactory one, it has been used to account for Brick's malaise just as Hamlet's disgust has been explained as a reaction to his incestuous desires for his mother. Similar explanations have been given for Claggart's mysterious hatred for Billy Budd in Melville's novella and Gustave Aschenbach's degeneration in Mann's *Death in Venice*. In fact, much of the metaphysical mystery of the so-called southern Gothic school of literature, a group in which Williams is often placed, has similarly been attributed to suppressed homosexuality, incest, pederasty, and other sexual "perversions."

That such explanations miss the point quite a bit more than they hit it is suggested by Williams in his introduction to the New Directions edition of Carson McCullers' *Reflections in a Golden Eye*. In this mock dialogue with a puzzled representative of the "everyday humdrum world" in which Williams compares the southern Gothic writers to the French existentialists, he also gives us a clue to the metaphysical mystery of Brick Pollitt. The true sense of dread in life, says Williams, is "not reaction to anything sensible or visible or even, strictly, materially, *knowable*. But rather it's a kind of spiritual intuition of something almost too incredible and shocking to talk about, which underlies the whole so-called thing. It is the incommunicable something that we shall have to call mystery." Brick's detachment is an existential leveling of values that makes no one thing more important than another. It is the result of an awareness of absurdity that, as Albert Camus says, can come at any time with no discernible cause and that resists any attempts at psychological explanation. Like Hamlet who senses that the rottenness in Denmark reflects a rottenness at the heart of existence, Brick is existentially aware of the universality of the mendacity on Big Daddy's plantation kingdom, and in face of it he too would wish that his too solid flesh would melt.

However, whereas Hamlet cannot find anything to do that is adequate to resolve the disgust he feels, Brick no longer tries to do anything. This withdrawn impassivity, Brick's refusal to act, even to think, makes his basic situation difficult for the reader to understand. When a fictional character faces a problem that he cannot articulate, a problem that evades attempts to conceptualize it, perhaps the only way the artist can communicate the nature of the problem is to show how the character attempts to deal with it. Thus, the "inadmissible thing" that lies at the heart of *Oedipus* cannot be presented directly. Rather, the play unfolds as a series of attempts by Oedipus to resolve a problem which, while symbolically objectified by the plague, truly hides within metaphysical mysteries that evade all "pat conclusions" and "facile definitions."

Ernest Hemingway, who was always concerned with the artistic problem of finding objective correlatives for the sense of metaphysical dread that Williams calls an "incommunicable something that we shall have to call mystery," also found that he could best present it by objectifying the attempts of his characters to deal with it. For example, in "A Clean, Well-Lighted Place," there is no objective correlative adequate to the old waiter's sense of nada which has seized him. However, the clean, well-lighted place itself is a communicable symbol of a way to live with that sense of nada. Similarly, the mysterious fear and dread that have taken hold of Nick Adams in "Big Two-Hearted River" is not adequately objectified by the "tragic" nature of the swamp, but the way to deal with the dread is adequately communicated by the detailing of Nick's fishing activities that make up the story.

However, in *Cat on a Hot Tin Roof*, because Brick makes no effort to deal with his problem, we are given no clues as to the nature of Brick's problem via an objectification of a possible solution or even, as in Hemingway's stories, a possible palliative. The click in his head that Brick drinks to achieve seems merely an intensification of his already withdrawn state. It gives no hint of why he wishes to withdraw. And, as noted, Brick's disgust seems to exceed its ostensible cause as objectified by the relationship with Skipper. The result is that while a great deal of action goes on around Brick in the play, action which reveals the motives of the other characters, Brick remains inactive and thus unrevealed.

I suggest that Williams does not have Brick make any effort to resolve his problem in *Cat on a Hot Tin Roof* because in an earlier fictional account of the dilemma Brick does make such an effort, the only kind of effort that can be made, and it is inevitably doomed to fail. Tom S. Reck, in an essay on the relationship between Williams' stories and plays, suggests that "Three Players of a Summer Game," published in *The New Yorker* only two years before Williams wrote *Cat*, may come closer to the "whole truth" about Brick than the play does. However, Reck makes no more effort than any of the other critics to determine what that whole truth is.

The truth is certainly not to be found in the ostensible cause for Brick's disgust given in the story, for that is left even more mysterious than in the play. Williams' story-telling narrator says only that his "self-disgust came upon him with the abruptness and violence of a crash on a highway. But what had Brick crashed into? Nothing that anybody was able to surmise, for he seemed to have everything that young men like Brick might hope or desire to have." The only strictly "knowable" thing suggested in the story that might be the cause of Brick's "dropping his life and taking hold of a glass which he never let go of for more than one waking hour" is, as it is in *Cat*, a sexual problem—in this case, his emasculation by his wife Margaret and a consequent sexual impotence. This is hinted at in Brick's drunken monologue to the house painters in which, "explaining things to the world," he is, as he also is in *Cat*, "like an old-time actor in a tragic role," telling as much as he knows of the Truth: "the meanest thing one human being can do to another human being is to take his respect for himself away from him. . . . I had it took away from me! I won't tell you how, but maybe, being men about my age, you're able to guess it. That was how. Some of them don't want it. They cut it off. They cut it right off a man, and half the time he don't even know when they cut it off him. Well, I knew it all right. I could feel it being cut off me." A bit later Brick continues the castration allusion by explaining how he is going to solve his drinking problem. "I'm not going to take no cure and I'm not going to take no pledge, I'm just going to prove I'm a man with his balls back on him!"

The irony and seeming contradiction of trying to prove one's masculinity by learning to play what Brick himself calls the "sissy" game of croquet should be hint enough that Brick's problem is not emasculation and impotence in the psychosexual sense in which we usually understand such terms. Rather as in *Cat*, Brick's problem is a more basic and pervasive one for which his sexual dilemma is merely a symbolic objectification. The complexity of the problem can best be seen by examining the way Brick seeks to deal with it, that is, by examining the summer game itself—both the purely aesthetic game of croquet and the psychological game Brick plays with the other two players, the young widow Isabel and her daughter Mary Louise. Brick's impotence is not a reaction against the emasculating

Margaret, but rather a revolt against the flesh itself. His flight into the chaste, because death-purified, arms of Isabel is the search for Truth in its Keatsean equation with Beauty. It is an attempt to escape from flesh into art, to escape from the intolerable, because contingent, real into the bearable, because detached and fleshless, ideal of artistic form.

However, this attempt to escape the contingency of existence by means of aesthetic patterning and idealizing is doomed from the start, for Brick's hoped-for ideal relationship with Isabel as well as his effort to play the superior game of art and form with human beings as counters comes crashing against the "real" fleshly and psychological needs of the other two players. The problem is similar to the one facing Aschenbach in *Death in Venice*. He, too, wishing for the form and detachment of Beauty, finds that unless it is embodied in the flesh it is inhuman; but if it is human, it must therefore be fleshly and consequently be that very thing from which he wishes to escape. It is this intolerable aesthetic and metaphysical dilemma that destroys him.

Tennessee Williams offers several suggestions throughout "Three Players of a Summer Game" that this indeed is the inadmissible, because unnamable, thing that so plagues Brick. At the end of the major events of the story, after Brick has realized the impossibility of his summer game and no longer comes to the widow's house, the narrator says, "The summer had spelled out a word that had no meaning, and the word was now spelled out and, with or without any meaning, there it was, inscribed with as heavy a touch as the signature of a miser on a check or a boy with chalk on a fence." Any attempt to "spell out" the problem, even the attempt the story itself makes, is inadequate to get at the Truth. However, even as the attempt to escape from life through art is the subject of the story, art is the only means to present such a subject; for it is a subject that must be presented obliquely and metaphorically through symbolic objectifications.

At the very beginning of the story the narrator establishes the metaphor that identifies the summer game with the nature of the art work, and he does so in language that Williams later uses in *Cat on a Hot Tin Roof* to refer to that "fiercely charged!—interplay of live human beings" that he wishes to capture in the play—"flickering, evanescent." The game of croquet itself, says the narrator, "seems, in a curious way, to be composed of images the way that a painter's abstraction of summer or one of its games would be built of them. The delicate wire wickets set in a lawn of smooth emerald that flickers fierily at some points and rests under violet shadows in others, the wooden poles gaudily painted as moments that stand out in a season that was a struggle for something of unspeakable importance to someone passing through it, the clean and hard wooden spheres of different colors and the strong rigid shape of the mallets that drive the balls through the wickets, the formal design of those wickets and poles upon the croquet lawn—all of these are like a painter's abstraction of a summer and a game played in it."

Likewise the characters in the story become images and abstractions, not so much real people as stylized gestures which are pictorially woven within the lyrical narrative that make up the "legend" of Brick Pollitt. The narrator is well aware that he is playing the game of detachment of form, the rule-bound ritualized game of arranging images in a formal design that both reveals and conceals the game of art. "These bits and pieces, these assorted images, they are like the paraphernalia for a game of croquet, gathered up from the lawn when the game is over and packed carefully into an oblong wooden box which they just exactly fit and fill. There they all are, the bits and pieces, the images, the apparently incongruous paraphernalia of a summer that was the last one of my childhood, and now I take them out of the oblong box and arrange them once more in the formal design on the lawn. It would be absurd to pretend that this is altogether the way it was, and yet it may be closer than a literal history could be to the hidden truth of it."

This engagement in the formally controlled, ritualized patterning of the art work that one plays to deal with the incongruity and contingency of life is of course the same game Brick wishes to play. The croquet game means the same kind of control to Brick that the fishing trip does to Nick Adams in "Big Two-Hearted River." As Brick explains to the painters and thus to the world, croquet is a wonderful game for a drinker. "You hit the ball through one wicket and then you drive it through the next one. . . . You go from wicket to wicket, and it's a game of precision—it's a game that takes concentration and precision, and that's what makes it a wonderful game for a drinker." The game for both Brick and the narrator of "Three Players of a Summer Game" is thus an Apollonian means to deal with the Dionysian drunkenness and incongruity of raw existential reality.

Although the relationship between the process of art and the process of game has often been noted, it has perhaps been given its most profound treatment in Johan Huizinga's *Homo Ludens: A Study of the Play Element in Culture*. Huizinga says that engagement in both play and art involves the assertion of freedom, the abolition of the ordinary world, and the participation in an action that is limited in time and space. In both the game and the art work, something invisible and inchoate takes form and transcends the bounds of logical and deliberative judgment. As Huizinga says, "All poetry is born of play. . . . What poetic language does with images is to play with them. It disposes them in style, it instills mystery into them so that every image contains the answer to an enigma." However, as Huizinga suggests, it is not the psychological meaning of the action that reveals the answer to the enigma, but rather the ritualized pattern that is formed from the bits and pieces, the actions and images, that make up the art work. It is this spatial-izing of the temporal, the transforming of the historical into myth, that the narrator of Williams' story says may come closer to the hidden truth of Brick Pollitt's summer game than a literal history.

That the summer game Brick plays with Isabel and her daughter is bound up with his own aesthetic search for detachment and form, his search for an escape from the temporal into the spatial, can be seen in what he desires of the relationship with Isabel. Williams must have had Keats stirring about in his mind when he wrote "Three Players of a Summer Game," for Keatsean aesthetic motifs echo throughout. Even the name Isabel and the fact that Isabel's husband's illness begins in a shocking way in which "An awful flower grew in his brain like a fierce geranium that shattered its pot" suggests Keats's Isabella and her beloved but gruesome pot of basil. Just as in Keats's poem, in Williams' story, hoped-for love and beauty germinate in death itself and remain inextricably tied to the horrors of the flesh.

Brick is initially drawn to Isabel because her actual encounter with the contingency and horror of flesh reflects his own metaphysical encounter. As together they watch the young doctor die, "*God* was the only word she was able to say; but Brick Pollitt somehow understood what she meant by that word, as if it were in a language that she and he, alone of all people, could speak and understand." After Brick pumps the death-delivering contents of the hypodermic needle into the doctor's arm, he and Isabel consummate their communion of metaphysical despair by lying together chastely in bed, "and the only movement between them was the intermittent, spasmodic digging of their fingernails into each other's clenched palm while their bodies lay stiffly separate, deliberately not touching at any other points as if they abhorred any other contact with each other, while this intolerable thing was ringing like an iron bell through them." The summer game thus becomes, says the narrator, a "running together out of something unbear-ably hot and bright into something obscure and cool"; it is the running out of the hot, unbearable world of existential reality into the cool, obscure world of the art work.

However, when Brick realizes, as does Gustave Aschenbach, that form must inevitably become involved and entangled with the reality of flesh, he finds himself caught on the horns of an unresolvable metaphysical dilemma. Thus, in "Three Players of a Summer Game," the ideal game of art as Huizinga describes it becomes enmeshed with the real game of existential reality as it has recently been analyzed by Eric Berne in *Games People Play*. Because two other players are involved in Brick's game, players who have real fleshly, emotional, and psychological needs, the game is contaminated when it must be played at the expense of Isabel and Mary Louise. Brick's motive for his game, concealed by its metaphysical and inchoate nature, results in the "real world" of the story in what Berne calls an "ulterior transaction" in which others are exploited by the player. Thus, the artistic game, at the same time that it is the most noble and ideal of all games, becomes a "substitute for the real living of real intimacy" as Berne says most of our social games are.

The exploitation is made quite clear in its effect on Mary Louise, lonely already because of the "cushions of flesh" which her mother promises will "dissolve in two or three more years," who is made even more lonely during the summer by being shut out of the house when Brick is there. However, as the summer passes, it also becomes apparent that Brick's need to play the artistic game of inhuman form is not satisfying to Isabel either. Although the conflict between Brick's ideal and Isabel's flesh is suggested in various ways in the story, the scene that makes it most obvious occurs one evening when, after setting up the croquet set, Mary Louise stands beneath her mother's bedroom window and wails for her and Brick to come out and play: "Almost immediately after the wailing voice was lifted, begging for the commence-ment of the game, Mary Louise's thin pretty mother showed herself at the window. She came to the window like a white bird flying into some unno-ticed obstruction. That was the time when I saw, between the dividing gauze of the bedroom curtains, her naked breasts, small and beautiful, shaken like two angry fists by her violent motion. She leaned between the curtains to answer Mary Louise not in her usual tone of gentle remonstrance but in a shocking cry of rage: 'Oh, be still, for God's sake, you fat little monster!'" The imagery of flight into an unexpected obstruction and the breasts like fists suggest the frustratingly unyielding obstruction her own flesh has met in Brick's gauzelike ideal.

The contrast between that ideal of the frozen art work that Brick desires and the real physical life that he must live with is perhaps indirectly suggested by an incident the narrator relates about a visit he and Mary Louise pay to an art museum. The scene may have more than accidental significance since it did not appear in the original version of the story in *The New Yorker*, but rather in the revised version that was published the following year in *Hard Candy*. When the two children enter a room with a reclining male nude entitled the "Dying Gaul," Mary Louise lifts the metal fig leaf from the bronze figure and turns to the narrator to ask, "Is yours like that?" Since the added incident has nothing directly to do with the problem of Brick, it may be another of the bits and pieces that reflect Brick's basic dilemma—being caught between the ideal Greek beauty of idealized body and the real and therefore ugly flesh of physical body.

Williams adds another passage to the *Hard Candy* version of the story. In the concluding description of Brick's being driven through the streets of town by Margaret, much the way a captured prince might be led through the streets of a capital city by his conqueror, Williams has the narrator describe him as the handsomest man you were likely to remember, adding significantly, "physical beauty being of all human attributes the most incontinently used and wasted, as if whoever made it despised it, since it is made so often only to be disgraced by painful degrees and drawn through the streets in chains." Thus, what Brick and the narrator learn in the story, although they learn it only in an inchoate and oblique way, is that when one uses human beings in an effort to play the game of art and reach the beauty and detachment of form, the result is the inevitable disgrace of the flesh. The beauty of the art work alone can remain pure, but only because of its inhumanness, its noninvolvement. Ike McCaslin's attempts to realize the Keatsean equation of Beauty and Truth in Faulkner's *Bear* by relinquishing all claims to the world and the flesh meet with the same ambiguous and inescapable paradox.

When Brick realizes the hopelessness of his aspiration, he is transformed from tragic actor to clown. The croquet lawn becomes a circus ring. Brick's tragicomic efforts come to a climax one night when he turns on the water sprinkler, takes off his clothes, and rolls about under the cascading arches. No longer the Greek statue, Brick is now "like some grotesque fountain figure, in underwear and necktie and the one remaining pale-green sock, while the revolving arch of water moved with cool whispers about him." The degeneration of the tragedy can also be seen in what the narrator calls a conclusion "declining into unintentional farce" as Isabel and Mary Louise carry on trivial conversations in the face of Brick's absence from the house. The conversation about the ice that Mary Louise uses to ease her mosquito bites is the culmination of a pervasive motif of frozen coolness interwoven throughout the story. A game that began with a running out of something hot into something obscure and cool, a game that took place among frozen stylized figures on the cool, dark lawn of a house that has the appearance of a block of ice, has now become a banal banter between "two ladies in white dresses waiting on a white gallery" in which the ice is reduced from its symbolic significance to the practical utility of cooling Brick's drinks, easing Mary Louise's mosquito bites, and putting in the ice bag for Isabel's headaches.

This analysis of how Brick attempts to deal with his problem in "Three Players of a Summer Game" should make clearer the metaphysical mystery of Brick's detachment in *Cat on a Hot Tin Roof*. The basic tension between the ideal and frozen art work and the unbearable hot tin roof of reality is the tension of both the story and the play. Even the "Person-to-Person" preface which Williams writes for *Cat* contains a clear reference to the problem of the Keatsean equation of Truth and Beauty that he is concerned with in the play. However, because Williams sees that such an equation is possible only in death or in the deathlike art work, the poem he chooses to reflect the dilemma is not from Keats, but from Emily Dickinson. In "I Died for Beauty," it is only in the grave that Beauty and Truth recognize that they are "brethren."

Perhaps one of the reasons for Williams' often expressed admiration for Maggie the Cat is that she alone in the play seems to realize what Brick's desire is. However, she also realizes that it means death and rejects it in her famous cry, "Maggie the cat is—*alive! I am alive, alive! I'm . . .—alive!*" Against Brick's protestations she tries to explain that she made love to Skipper only because of Brick's detachment, only because he refused to return the love of those who cared for him. "Skipper and I made love, if love you could call it, because it made both of us feel a little bit closer to you. You see, you son of a bitch, you asked too much of people, of me, of him, of all the unlucky poor damned sons of bitches that happen to love you . . . you— superior creature!—you godlike being!—And so we made love to each other to dream it was you, both of us! Yes, yes, yes! Truth, truth!" Maggie insists she does understand about Brick and Skipper, knows "It was one of those beautiful, ideal things they tell about in the Greek legends. . . . Brick, I tell you, you got to believe me, Brick, I *do* understand all about it! I—I think it was—*noble!* Can't you tell I'm sincere when I say I respect it? My only point, the only point that I'm making, is life has got to be allowed to continue even after the *dream* of life is—all—over. . . ."

It seems obvious that what Brick hoped to achieve in his games with Skipper is the same thing he aspired to in his croquet game with Isabel and Mary Louise, and it is also obvious that his effort fails for the same metaphysical reasons in both the story and the play: human needs always interfere with purely ideal aspirations. As a result, in *Cat* Brick stops playing altogether, or at least thinks he does; however, the click he waits to hear in his head is a metaphoric echo of the click of the croquet mallets that can be faintly heard offstage in act one. Maggie understands Brick's game-playing posture when she tells him he has always had a detached quality as though he were playing a game without much concern over whether he won or lost. Now that he has quit playing, she says he has the "charm of the defeated.— You look so cool, so cool, so enviably cool."

However, everything is not so cool for Brick, or else he would not continue to drink and wait for the click in his head; he would not stare out the window at the moon in act three and envy it for being a cool son of a bitch. Brick continues to try to play the ideal game in which the goal is not to win or lose, but rather to carry the game through. This time, though, he tries to play it alone. As Huizinga says, the essence of play can be summed up in the phrase, "There is something at stake"; yet this something is not the material result of the play, but rather the "ideal fact that the game is a success or has been successfully concluded." Now, however, Brick's problem is that the human games of others are always breaking in on the ideal game of cool withdrawal he wishes to play. If it is not what Maggie calls the "cardsharp" games of Gooper and Mae as they use their children as counters to win the legacy of Big Daddy, it is Maggie's own game of attempted seduction of Brick. The most pervasive game, however, that surrounds the action of the play and threatens to shatter Brick's detachment, is summarized in an offhand phrase by the insensitive Reverend Tooker as a game of life and death in which "the Stork and the Reaper are running neck and neck!"

In *Cat on a Hot Tin Roof*, Brick's game of detachment is as destructive and exploitative as his more directly involved game in "Three Players." This time Brick preserves his "charming detachment" by that "simple expedient" of not loving anyone enough to disturb it. Consequently, he damages Skipper, Maggie, and Big Daddy, all who need his love and involvement. However, as much as Brick realizes these needs, he can do nothing to satisfy them without entangling himself in the chaos of that real life that so disgusts him. He intuits that love of another human being not only is insufficient to fulfill the ideal demands of the human spirit; by its very nature such a love negates the possibility of such fulfilment. Perhaps it is this realization that made Williams object to the change Kazan wanted effected in Brick in the third act. In the original version of the play, when Maggie makes her announcement that she is pregnant, Brick simply keeps quiet, not as an attempt to save Maggie's face, but rather as a result of his own continued indifference. In the stage version, Brick actively supports Maggie's false claim, as if it truly makes a difference to him. His last words in the Broadway version are: "I admire you, Maggie." The implication is that he has found a solution to his problem and will henceforth be "alive" as Maggie says she is. The conclusion to the original version of the play is more ambiguous. As Maggie turns out the lights in the bedroom and the curtain begins to fall slowly, she says to Brick, "Oh, you weak people, you weak, beautiful people! —who give up. —What you want is someone to— . . . take hold of you.—Gently, gently, with love! And—. . . I *do* love you, Brick, I *do!*" Brick's final words before the curtain falls are uttered with that charming sad smile still on his face: "Wouldn't it be funny if that was true?" This final question of the play is not just in response to Maggie's declaration of love, but rather it is a fittingly enigmatic and ironic response to Maggie's claim that all such people as Brick need to resolve their metaphysical dilemma is for someone to take hold of them with love. Brick's final skeptical query then bears a striking resemblance in its hopeless ambiguity to Jake Barnes' reply to Lady Britt at the conclusion of Hemingway's *The Sun Also Rises*: "Isn't it pretty to think so?"

It is thus with Brick's mysterious metaphysical problem still unresolved that Tennessee Williams wished to end his play, for it is a problem that is not knowable by any ordinary epistemology nor solvable by any ordinary psychology. In "Three Players of a Summer Game," Isabel is obliquely referring to Brick when she responds to Mary Louise's question about why the sun goes south: "Precious, Mother cannot explain the movements of the heavenly bodies, you know that as well as Mother knows it. Those things are controlled by certain mysterious laws that people on earth don't know or understand."

ROGER BOXILL

Cat on a Hot Tin Roof

> BRICK POLLITT: Time just outran me, Big Daddy—
> got there first.

The first production of *Cat on a Hot Tin Roof* opened in 1955 at the Morosco Theatre in New York. It was directed by Elia Kazan with Ben Gazzara as Brick, Barbara Bel Geddes as Margaret, and Burl Ives as Big Daddy. The set and lighting were by Jo Mielziner. The 1958 London production was directed by Peter Hall with Paul Massie as Brick, Kim Stanley as Margaret, and Leo McKern as Big Daddy. The 1958 screen version was written by James Poe and Richard Brooks, and directed by Richard Brooks with Paul Newman, Elizabeth Taylor and Burl Ives. The 1974 New York revival was directed by Michael Kahn with Keir Dullea, Elizabeth Ashley and Fred Gwynne. A television adaptation was produced in 1976 with Robert Wagner, Natalie Wood and Laurence Olivier, and another in 1984 with Tommy Lee Jones, Jessica Lange and Rip Torn.

The story of *Cat on a Hot Tin Roof* begins with Jack Straw and Peter Ochello, a homosexual couple who in 1910 took in a young vagrant by the name of Pollitt to help them run their cotton plantation in the Mississippi Delta. As the estate grew, Pollitt rose to become overseer, then Ochello's partner after Straw's death, and finally sole owner after Ochello's. At twenty-five he took a wife (Ida), who bore him two sons, eight years apart. He hated

From *Tennessee Williams.* © 1987 by Roger Boxill.

the first (Gooper) but loved the second (Brick). By the time they were in college, Pollitt, who had left school at ten, was a multi-millionaire known as Big Daddy to his family, and the plantation stretched over 28,000 acres of rich Delta soil.

The son he hated was a success in the world at thirty-five, the son he loved a has-been at twenty-seven. Gooper became a lawyer, married well and had five children. The handsome Brick, an athletic star in college, became an alcoholic after a short-lived career as a professional football-player and sports announcer. He had taken, reluctantly, a wife of shabby genteel background (Margaret), who held only a lukewarm attraction for him. Even before their marriage he was far more interested in a fellow athlete (Skipper), with whom he imagined he had a 'pure' relationship. When the wife, who soon began to feel like the cat in the title, called the friend to account, he tried to reveal his hidden desire to the husband. Brick would not listen. The rejected Skipper died soon thereafter of drugs and alcohol, and Brick stopped sleeping with Margaret. Holding her responsible for his friend's ruin gave him a reason for no longer engaging in intimacies toward which he had been indifferent from the start.

At about the same time Big Daddy Pollitt stopped sleeping with Ida. In the five-odd years since then he developed terminal cancer. When the play begins, however, he does not yet know the grim prognosis. Indeed, both he and Ida (Big Mama) have been told that, on the contrary, the results of all the recent tests were negative. The enacted events, which are continuous, take place on Big Daddy's birthday in and about the plantation house at which his family have gathered. Gooper, afraid that his father will leave him nothing, has a plan in his briefcase to get control of the estate. Brick, having tried to jump the hurdles at his old high school the previous night, hobbles about on a crutch with one foot in a cast.

In this dramatic elegy the dying father yields his world to the defeated son. Act I shows the non-marriage of the frustrated Margaret and the detached Brick. Act II is the confrontation of Big Daddy and Brick in which the former learns that he is dying and the latter that he is guilty of complicity in the death of his friend for refusing to face the question of homosexuality with him. In Act III Margaret declares that she is pregnant, and, whether or not she can make the lie come true, it is evident that she and Brick will inherit the estate.

There are four published versions of Act III, two of which—the original and the Broadway—are printed in *Theatre*, III (1971) with a note by Williams explaining that the second was written for the premiere production under the prompting of its director, Elia Kazan. In the Broadway version Big Daddy reappears to tell a bawdy joke, thereby showing that he will face death with Pantagruelian equanimity. When Margaret tells him that she is pregnant, he says he wants his lawyer in the morning, proof of confidence that he can now leave his land to his chosen seed. Brick himself shows signs of rehabilitation by openly supporting Margaret in her lie before the suspicious Gooper and his wife (Mae). Perhaps it will come true that very night. When Margaret, having thrown out all the liquor, tells Brick she will get more if he satisfies her desire, he says he admires her. In the play's last moments she kneels at the foot of the bed and vows that she is determined to restore him to life.

In the original version Big Daddy does not reappear. Nor does Brick support Margaret in her lie. But neither does he say anything to put it in question. Big Mama goes to tell her husband the consoling news. We know from her response to it that Brick ('my son, Big Daddy's boy! Little Father!') will be the heir. When Margaret, having locked up the liquor, tells Brick she will take it out again once he satisfies her desire, he says there is nothing to say. In the play's last moments she insists that she loves him, and Brick, in the same phrase his father used when his mother protested as much to her husband, replies, 'Wouldn't it be funny if that was true?' The version used in the 1974 revival is like the original except that Big Daddy reappears to tell his joke. The acting-version is like the Broadway except that the joke is cut.

Although in his *Memoirs* Williams takes pride in *Cat* as a drama of which Aristotle would have approved, no version of Act III quite works, because the final act is an afterthought. Admittedly, the time span is diurnal in *Cat*, as opposed to seasonal in *Menagerie, Summer and Smoke* and *Streetcar*, but this has less to do with Aristotle than with the fact that *Cat* is one of Williams's story-telling plays. It is close in form to *Night of the Iguana*, closer still to the mid-length *Small Craft Warnings*, and closest of all to the better-known mid-length *Suddenly Last Summer*, in which, as in *Cat*, a story (containing the suicide of a young homosexual) is narrated within a dramatic frame that leaves room for the comic relief of a squabble over inheritance by grasping relatives.

The elegiac figure of Big Daddy Pollitt towers over *Cat* like a colossus. The dying of the same light against which he rages, scenic and symbolic, gathers about the legendary old salesman of the Delta in *The Last of my Solid Gold Watches*, Charlie Colton, as he speaks from his heart about the world which has passed him by to his unsympathetic young colleague. In *Cat* Williams again uses the device he perfected in his early one-act plays, that of a character telling his story to poor critical reception. Margaret's long speeches in Act I give an account of herself and her marriage that her husband can barely stand to hear. Big Daddy's earnest performance in Act II prompts his deeply troubled son more than once to stop him. When it is Brick's turn to tell his own story, his father responds by calling him a liar.

Cat is two duologues (I–II) and an ensemble (III). The duologues are essentially monologues. Because the drama is over at the end of the second, the ensemble is an appendage to them. It contains no intrigue because the playwright is interested not in plot but in the revelation of character through confrontation. It contains no suspense because it is a foregone conclusion that the favoured son, a repressed homosexual, will inherit the estate, and another that he will never get over the loss of his youth. In the scene between the hard father and the soft son Williams did everything that he had wanted to do with Brick and Big Daddy. But theatrical convention demanded a longer play, and, as the playwright tells us in his explanatory note, his director asked that Big Daddy not be left out of it, that Margaret be made more sympathetic, and that Brick show some sign of change for the better. According to Peter Hoffman, Williams said that revising Act III to please Kazan 'ruined' him as a writer because it prevented him from dealing honestly with Brick's homosexuality. Yet, while it is true that the Broadway version goes straight for the Happy Ending, the original is only a notch less sentimental and the script of the 1974 revival compromises between the two. When all is said and done, the stage versions are not much more convincing than the screenplay, in which the hero resumes sexual relations with his wife as soon as his problem—that of inadequate paternal love—has been solved by a heart-to-heart talk with his father.

On a deep level, of course, that is just the trouble with Brick. It is because the playwright lacked—or felt he lacked—his father's approval in life that he endowed the favoured son in *Cat* with the attributes of both his male and his female masks. In Brick Pollitt the wanderer and the faded belle begin to coalesce. The 'godlike' ex-football-star, a victim of time under thirty, instead of being a wayfarer is a recluse like Laura Wingfield, to whose physical handicap his present injury corresponds. His alcoholism and his privileged birth ally him with Blanche DuBois. Indeed it is, his puritan 'disgust' with homosexuality, no less than Blanche's, that results in the analogous loss by suicide of his closest human tie. Blanche and Brick, as the symbolic white they wear reminds us, had both wished for a kind of marriage of pure souls. The presently withdrawn Brick is a measure of the early Blanche. If her later promiscuity throws further light on the hero, his homosexuality cannot be closeted for long.

As Arthur Ganz has shrewdly observed, what Williams did in *Cat* was to pull *Streetcar* inside out. The beautiful dream of the past appears to unfold in the fabulous reality of the present. Antebellum splendour lost to decadence is regained by paternal endeavour. Instead of a small apartment in an urban slum, we see an enormous bedsitting-room through whose huge double doors a white balustrade indicates the upstairs gallery of a great plantation house. Rather than a hostile exterior encroaching upon a narrow interior, we are confronted by a commodious living-space roofed by the sky and reaching out into a peaceful beyond. Proletarian 'types' are replaced by professional gentlemen, vendors and prostitutes by friendly servants and singing field hands, poker at night with its potential for violence by the leisurely pastime of croquet in the afternoon.

Exposure and eviction, devastating in *Streetcar*, are merely idle threats in *Cat*. It soon becomes obvious that the hero will come into his father's kingdom despite the fertility and chicanery of the comic in-laws. Sexual assault is also reduced to a gesture. At the end of *Streetcar*, the carnal Stanley, dressed in red silk pyjamas, makes Blanche the 'tiger' drop the bottle top and bends her to his will. At the beginning of *Cat*, the celibate Brick, dressed in white silk pyjamas, wards off Maggie the cat's amorous advance by holding a boudoir chair between them like a lion-tamer.

Although in the drama of body and soul the sexes are reversed, it is Big Daddy Pollitt with his physical appetite, rough eloquence and imposing authority who reminds us most of Stanley Kowalski. Both powerful men, adored by their wives, smash through the pretensions of gentility or ritual around them with bare-knuckled realism. But, instead of being the heroine's enemy, Big Daddy is the hero's ally. Whereas in *Streetcar* the rough man ruins the heroine's birthday, in *Cat* he ruins his own—for those about him. He reserves his greatest scorn for his wife, whose pathetic efforts to make the party a success prove vain. Analogously, Margaret fails to get Brick to enter into the spirit of things. Whereas Blanche's present is a notice of eviction, Big Daddy's—all he wanted—is the promise of his favourite son's paternity.

The counterpoint of life and death should seem more hopeful in *Cat*. The removal of Blanche coincides with the appearance of Stella's baby, just as the prognosis of Big Daddy's death coincides with the announcement of Margaret's pregnancy. In *Streetcar* the birth is a step down, in *Cat* a step up. Stanley's fatherhood is associated with rape, Margaret's motherhood with the outflanking of Mae and Gooper. Whereas in the first case the apes take over, in the second the dogs are held at bay.

Streetcar contemplates an end, *Cat* a beginning. Blanche gives Stanley the bunch of old papers to which debauchery has reduced Belle Reve. Big Daddy gives Brick the Straw and Ochello estate that his own labours have built into a kingdom. Homosexuality is linked to the creation of the plantation instead of to its loss. It is true that in both plays a suicide has aborted a marriage. But the 'degenerate' Allan Grey as the husband of the last DuBois owner belongs to the final phase in a history of slow decay. The 'tender' homosexual love between Jack Straw and Peter Ochello belongs to the initial phase in a history of rapid growth. It is in their very bedroom, moreover, in a setting described as evocative of their benign ghosts, that the present heir, himself a homosexual, is closeted.

Yet, if *Cat* contemplates a beginning, it is the beginning of the end. Big Daddy is dying. The real ruin of the festive occasion is his son's angry announcement to him of the terrible truth that on the anniversary of his birth he must prepare for his death. Nor is Brick likely, despite his protective wife, in his father's house to build more stately mansions. The anxiety of the titular heroine, the result of sexual frustration, already begins to ally her with the faded belle. Her relation to her detached and self-destructive husband is like those in which the belle, or anyhow a character resembling her, tries in vain to save the foredoomed wanderer. There is serious doubt whether the 'frantic' Margaret can keep Brick Pollitt from drinking himself into the grave like his friend Skipper before him.

Margaret drives Brick to drink in 'Three Players of a Summer Game', the short story from which the play derives. There is no Big Daddy and no Skipper, unless the two characters may be said to exist embryonically in the young cancer victim (by the telling name of Grey) with whose widow, Isabel, Brick has a summer affair in the vain attempt to escape from his emasculating wife. The game is croquet, and its three players are Brick, Isabel and her twelve-year-old daughter, Mary Louise, with whom the narrator was friends in the last summer of his childhood. At the end of the story, Williams emphasises the castration theme by comparing Margaret to an ancient conqueror as she drives about town with her amiably senseless husband like a captive in chains behind her. He also defines it by the mortification that the narrator remembers feeling as a boy when Mary Louise lifted the fig leaf off a male nude in a sculpture gallery and, turning to him, asked ingenuously, 'Is yours like that?'

That this incident took place between Williams and Hazel Kramer (it is recorded in his *Memoirs*) reminds us once more of how close the author's psychological life is to his work. What Margaret refers to in *Cat* as Brick's coolness toward sex may ultimately have its root in Williams's fear of castration. Whether it does or not, it is clear that, from an autobiographical standpoint, the play is a wishful fantasy in which Williams receives his father's approval and then kills him. Indeed, he enjoys the preference of both parents over his more worldly brother (a lawyer, like Dakin), whom he turns into a grasper and a fool. He is at the centre of attention by what amounts to natural right: admired while doing nothing to deserve admiration and sexually irresistible while remaining aloof. He creates a friend who commits suicide for the love of him and a wife who says she would do so too if she ever lost hope that he would once more make love to her with the 'indifference' she so rapturously recalls. By making the wife and the friend go to bed together for what Margaret at one point says is the purpose of dreaming of him, the puritan and the cavalier Williams has his cake and eats it too, preserving his goodness while being passionately desired.

The myth of the Old South merges with the longing for a return to spotless childhood in a summer reverie of white and gold. But the longing, like the myth, based on fantasy rather than fact, turns out to be equally vain. Brick is a child in a world of adults, sharing a room, if not a bed, with a maternally protective young woman. He is burdened with the death-like security that Williams says in 'A Streetcar Named Success' came with achieving the 'absolute protection and utter effortlessness' that the 'homesick little boy' in him had always wanted. Significant people and places in the child's dreaming mind—Daddy, Mama, house, plantation—are all big. The late-afternoon sun, filtered through bamboo shades, casts gold-fretted shadows over the big room and across the snowy surface of the big bed that dominates it. A look of benign age, as if of wicker furniture outdoors for many seasons, governs the 'gently and poetically haunted' space where the handsome couple appear in the chaste yet seductive garb of dream life, she in a slip of ivory satin and lace, he in white silk pyjamas.

The child's dream cannot satisfy the man. Nor can the idealistic dream of youth endure beyond life's brief period of bloom. The appearance of the hero with his cast and his crutch defines his role as time's victim. Feelings of immortality and limitless potential have dispersed with the experience of age. Brick's homosexuality and his self-deception regarding it are secondary to his discovery that the 'dream of life' is over. He drinks, he tells his father, because he no longer 'believes'. The end of the romance of his friendship and the end of his athletic career have taught him that he is neither a 'pure' nor an ageless being but a creature of frail flesh already defeated in the futile race with time.

The first production stressed the play's dreamlike quality. On walking into the Morosco theatre, one noticed the point or corner of a raked plat-form extending past the scrim at the proscenium line, sloping down over the pit like the prow of a plunging ship, and reaching into the house itself, where the first two rows of orchestra seats had been replaced by settees. There was no curtain. When the house lights dimmed, horizontal bars of alternating light and shade were projected on the scrim from the balcony rail. As the first words were spoken, up-stage lighting faded in to reveal Jo Mielziner's full set: an enormous room with soaring jalousies at the far end that the projections on the transparent scrim, which was now slowly opening, had suggested. There were no walls or doors. An ornate fresco with two plump cupids decorated the floating canopy above. A catwalk suggested a balcony outside the windows. The console liquor cabinet was up left. The bed was up centre, its high wicker headboard twisted into an elaborate cornucopia motif.

In the beginning, shifting clouds and shadows, later stars and fireworks, were visible through the open jalousies, projected images on a cyclorama under which mirroring suggested the surface of an adjacent pond or stream. A gauze curtain in front of the cyclorama enhanced the illusion of depth. In the code phrase of Century Lighting, which supplied the equipment for the production, the scenes were 'painted with light'. The sunset colours with which Act I began gave way to the pale moonlight of Act III. During key scenes the general lighting was dimmed or even turned out completely as actors worked in follow spots trained on them from the balcony.

Elia Kazan's ceremonial blocking was part of the anti-naturalistic conception. Actors changed position like figures in a drill and stood in formal groups as if posing for pictures. They sometimes held position for as long as ten beats. These effects made perceptive critics such as Eric Bentley and Henry Hewes think of film. The arrested action was analogous to the freeze frame just as the follow spot was to the close-up. Despite the audacious theatricality of the set, lighting and directing, the acting of individual roles was marked by the detail and intensity of the neo-Stanislavskyan American Method. Ben Gazzara's sullen, mumbling Brick was within the Actors Studio tradition established by Marlon Brando's Stanley Kowalski. Barbara Bel Geddes's golden Margaret matched in sincerity his deep concentration. The corpulent Burl Ives, best known as a folk singer, gave to the profane, waggish and wrathful Big Daddy the appearance of solid reality.

If truth to nature lay just under the deliberate artifice of the performance, the teeming life of the plantation lay just outside the magical space defined by the raked stage. The prompt-book for *Cat*, according to its production stage-manager, was 'a veritable scenario' of off-stage footsteps, birdcalls, songs and conversation. From time to time the blues of Brownie McGhee on guitar and Sonny Terry on harmonica could be heard faintly in the distance. The effect of the whole suggested the experience of the mind while in the condition of reverie when the events of the real world seem to lie just beyond the symbolic visions that float up from the unconscious.

The problem of playing *Cat* in 1955 was how much to make of Brick's homosexuality. The result was equivocation. That is why several critics were dissatisfied with the inconclusiveness of Ben Gazzara's Brick and what appeared to be his miraculous 'salvation' by Barbara Bel Geddes's shimmering Margaret. Watts of the *New York Post* had great trouble believing the happy conclusion. Eric Bentley blamed the director. Kerr of the *New York Herald-Tribune* took Williams to task for not making Brick's motives clear.

Yet Kerr, reviewing the 1974 revival for the *New York Times*, complimented the playwright with having known what he was about all along. It only took Keir Dullea's hysterical outbursts to show that the hero was protesting his virility too much. Elizabeth Ashley, furthermore, by stressing Margaret's feline tenacity, held the character back from the trap of sentimentality.

The problem of playing *Cat* today would be how to subordinate the dated topic of homosexuality to the perennial and overriding subject of loss in time. The key is the hero's likeness to his father. The reason for Brick's favoured position as 'son of Big Daddy' is that both men are close in spirit to an earlier and simpler America, or at least to the romance of one. The great self-made planter and the football idol are out of place in the modern corporate nation. The present belongs to the Goopers. The age of heroes is past. The plantation version of the agrarian myth thereby serves the elegiac theme. The action of the play is the passing of the father and the passing of the youth of the son. The father's end is near, the son's beginning is over. Brick, having peaked, has begun the slow process of dying which, in the playwright's view, constitutes the remainder of human life and demonstrates nature's passion for declivity.

JOHN M. CLUM

"Something Cloudy, Something Clear": Homophobic Discourse in Tennessee Williams

Throughout his career, Tennessee Williams was attacked from all sides for his treatment or nontreatment of homosexuality in his work. During the early years of gay liberation, gay critics complained that Williams was not "out" enough in his work and demanded that he stop writing around his homosexuality. One gay playwright went so far as to assert: "He has yet to contribute any work of understanding to gay theater." Williams's response to such attacks was a series of candid personal disclosures culminating in the unfortunate volume of memoirs, and more explicit treatment of homosexuality in his later, often autobiographical works. This new candor led to attacks by heterosexual critics, one of whom even referred to one play of the seventies as "faggotty fantasizing."

The first critic to deal intelligently with this aspect of Williams's work was Edward A. Sklepowitch, whose formulation was too simplistic, though typical of early work in gay studies:

> Williams' so-called "decadent" vision and his preoccupation with loneliness, evasion, role-playing, wastage, sexual reluctance and sexual excess are in many instances functions of a homosexual sensibility which has been evolving steadily in the more than quarter century since the publication of *One Arm and Other*

From *The South Atlantic Quarterly* 88, no. 1 (Winter 1989). © 1989 by Duke University Press.

Stories. In this period, Williams' treatment of homosexuality has undergone significant changes, moving from a mystical to a more social perspective, a personal, if fictional microcosm of the wider cultural demystification of homosexuality.

I do not see such a steady evolution in Williams's "homosexual sensibility": rather, there seems to be a constant attitude toward homosexual acts, though Williams's presentation of homosexual persons changed when public tolerance allowed a candidness in drama which Williams had previously restricted to his stories and poems. That change in presentation, alas, was also a function of his decreased ability to convert memory or self-judgment into a controlled work of art. But the constant in Williams's career is the dual vision that shaped his presentation of the homosexuality he was always impelled to write about.

Some relatively late statements issued by Williams demonstrate his sense of a split personality which separated the homosexual artist from his work, and they provide a crucial starting point for any discussion of the relation of Williams's sexual orientation to his work, particularly his plays. This one is from an interview with Dotson Rader:

> I never found it necessary to deal with it [homosexuality] in my work. It was never a preoccupation of mine, except in my intimate, private life.

Quibbling with this statement becomes a matter of semantics. Williams may not have found it "necessary" to "deal with" homosexuality in his work, but the fact is he did. His poetry is filled with homoerotic visions and encounters with "gentlemen callers." Indeed, no poet has so vividly and poignantly captured the tension, excitement, and loneliness of the anonymous sexual encounter as Williams, from the wry humor of "Life Story" to the poignancy of "Young Men Waking at Daybreak." The focus of these poems is not so much homo*sexuality* as it is the peculiar alienation of the brief sexual encounter. Williams's best stories also feature homosexuals as central characters. The semi-canonization of the boxer/hustler/murderer in "One Arm," who dies with love letters from the men with whom he has tricked jammed between his legs, is typical in its combination of religion, mortality, and impersonal gay sex which pervades many of Williams's best stories. The plays, too, are filled with homosexual characters: from the offstage martyrs of the plays of the major period, to the happy, ideal "marriage" of Jack Straw and Peter Ochello in *Cat on a Hot Tin Roof,* to the writers, artists, and hustlers of the later plays for whom sex is a temporary cure for loneliness.

Williams's theoretical separation of his homosexuality from his work is in conflict with his many assertions of the highly personal nature of his work and of his close relationship with his characters. It does not conform with "I draw all my characters from myself. I can't draw a character unless I know it within myself," unless one factors in an essential variable: "I draw every character out of my very multiple split personality." Split personality and split vision are recurring themes in Williams's work, particularly in references to himself. They suggest not only the multiple split personalities which allow such empathetic relationships with his characters, but also the split presentation of his own homosexuality.

Part of Williams's need to deny the homosexual element in his work is an extension of his need for validation as a writer (though he seldom got it in the last twenty-five years of his life). Admitting to the homosexual dimension of his work was a professional liability:

> You still want to know why I don't write a gay play? I don't find it necessary. I could express what I wanted to express through other means. I would be narrowing my audience a great deal [if I wrote for a gay audience alone]. I wish to have a broad audience because the major thrust of my work is not sexual orientation, it's social. I'm not about to limit myself to writing about gay people.

While making clear his continued, though frustrated, interest in writing for a broad audience, this statement demonstrates Williams's political naiveté: for him, homosexuality was merely a sexual issue, thus incongruent with his "social" interest. This separation is impossible for the homosexual, for whom the sexual *is* social, as Williams implies when he passionately asserts that "I do not deal with the didactic, ever." For him, a gay play was bound to be didactic, a notion his later work all too often bears out.

The split persona is seen again in a crucial quotation from his *Memoirs:* "Of course I also existed outside of conventional society while contriving somewhat precariously to remain in contact with it. For me this was not only precarious but a matter of dark unconscious disturbance." While Williams is referring to himself as a social being rather than as an artist, this statement defines the problematics of Williams's stance as homosexual artist and of the gulf between private art (poetry and fiction) and public art (drama), and the corollary gap between private homosexual and public celebrity. For most of his career, Williams was extremely protective of this split. Homosexuality was not the only element of Williams's personality which placed him outside of conventional society, but it was the subject which in the 1940s and 1950s seldom spoke its name. Williams was privately open about his sexual orientation, but publicly cautious, as he was relatively willing to treat homosexuality directly in his nondramatic writings, which would reach a limited audience (he never until his later years strove for the money and publicity of a best-selling novel), but cautious in his dramas. His caution takes two forms. One is the clever use of what he calls "obscurity or indirection" to soften and blur the homosexual element of much of his work. The other is a complex acceptance of homophobic discourse, which he both critiques and embraces.

This reliance on and occasional manipulation of the language of homophobia is the basis of Williams's treatment of the subject of homosexuality in his plays, reflecting a split he saw in his own nature. Williams wrote of his vision problems in 1940:

> My left eye was cloudy then because it was developing a cataract. But my right eye was clear. It was like the two sides of my nature: The side that was obsessively homosexual, compulsively interested in sexuality. And the side that in those days was gentle and understanding and contemplative.

This double vision, which always obsessed the playwright and led to the title of his last produced play in New York, *Something Cloudy, Something Clear*, defines the split Williams conceived between his homosexual activity and his "human" side. Even in his confused later novel, *Moise and the World of Reason*, in which he depicts himself as an eccentric aging playwright the narrator encounters, he fixes on a dual vision:

> He came back to the table and simultaneously two things happened of the automatic nature. He kissed me on the mouth and I started to cry. . . .
>
> "Baby, I didn't mean to do that, it was just automatic."
>
> (He thought I was crying over his Listerine kiss which I'd barely noticed.)
>
> He slumped there drinking the dago red wine as if to extinguish a fire in his belly, the rate at which he poured it down him slowing only when the bottle was half-empty. Then his one good eye focussed on me again but the luster was gone from it and its look was inward.

The outward gaze becomes linked to an automatic, impersonal homosexual advance while the inward gaze signifies the writer's now uncontrollable withdrawals into memory, which form the basis of his later autobiographical work which, paradoxically, depicts his split vision and at the same time demonstrates the loss his work suffered when he blurred the public/private split which was essential to his control over memory and craft.

Williams's split vision, then, defines the internal conflict that compelled him to write of his homosexuality and, in doing so, to rely on the language of indirection and homophobic discourse. It signified a cloudy sense of his own sexual identity, but it enabled him to write clearly. On the other hand, as the sexual self became clearer, and the plays became more autobiographical, the writing became murkier.

* * *

The story "Hard Candy" (1954), characteristic of Williams's fiction in dealing with homosexuality and its evasions, embodies Williams's split vision and attendant manipulation of language. "Hard Candy" centers on the last day in the life of an elderly man, Mr. Krupper, who habitually goes to an old movie palace with a bag of hard candy and a handful of quarters, his bribes to willing young men for their sexual favors. On the day of the story, Mr. Krupper dies while performing fellatio on a handsome young vagrant. Before describing Mr. Krupper's fatal visit to the movie theater, Williams offers this peculiar rejoinder:

> In the course of this story, and very soon now, it will be necessary to make some disclosures about Mr. Krupper of a nature *too coarse* to be dealt with very directly in a work of such brevity. The grossly naturalistic details of a life, contained in the enormously wide context of that life, are softened and qualified by it, but when you attempt to set those details down in a tale, *some measure of obscurity or indirection* is called for to provide the same, or even approximate, softening effect that existence in time gives to those gross elements in the life itself. When I say that there was a *certain mystery* in the life of Mr. Krupper, *I am beginning to approach those things in the only way possible without a head-on violence that would disgust and destroy and which would only falsify the story.*
>
> To have hatred and contempt for a person . . . calls for the assumption that you know practically everything of any significance about him. If you admit that he is a *mystery*, you admit that the hostility may be unjust.

Mr. Krupper's "mystery" is contained in his afternoon visits to the Joy Rio movie theater; his sexual encounters there with poor, beautiful (of course) young men are acts which would brand him in the eyes of most people as a "dirty old man" or worse. Williams's rejoinder both shows his sympathy and understanding of his audience's sensibilities and prejudices, and plays with those prejudices. The language of mystery and evasion allows him to write about the forbidden in a sympathetic, even subversive way. That mystery, however, is also clothed in harsh authorial judgment, which places the narrator in a superior position to his central character and allies him with the "average reader's" moral judgment. As Mr. Krupper approaches the Joy Rio theater, the narrator describes it as "the place where the mysteries of his nature are to be made unpleasantly manifest to us." Williams is both compassionate and judgmental: the story is both grotesque and touching. The "mysteries," however natural, are "unpleasant."

This dual vision functions in a number of ways in the story. There is the split between the physical grotesqueness and disease of the subject, which implies a connection between disease/ugliness and homosexual desire, and the shadowy beauty of the object of that desire. More important, the story embodies an intense consciousness of the split between the public persona and the private actor central to Williams's treatment of homosexuality:

> When around midnight the lights of the Joy Rio were brought up for the last time that evening, the body of Mr. Krupper was discovered in his remote box of the theater with his knees on the floor and his ponderous torso wedged between two wobbly gilt chairs as if he had expired in an attitude of prayer. The notice of the old man's death was given unusual prominence for the obituary of someone who had no public character and whose private character was so peculiarly low. But evidently the private character of Mr. Krupper was to remain anonymous in the memories of those anonymous persons who had enjoyed or profited from his company in the tiny box at the Joy Rio, for the notice contained no mention of anything of such a special nature. It was composed by a spinsterly reporter who had been impressed by the sentimental values of a seventy year old retired merchant dying of thrombosis at a cowboy thriller with a split bag of hard candies in his pocket and the floor about him littered with sticky wrappers, some of which even adhered to the shoulders and sleeves of his jacket.

Mr. Krupper dies in a public place while engaged in a very private act that is never in any way literally described in a story which is a model of playful circumspection. Yet the gay reader immediately recognizes the significance of Mr. Krupper's position and the act of worship it denotes, as he understands the sticky papers from the candies which are stuck to Mr. Krupper's shoulders and sleeves. Characteristically for Williams, an act of pederasty satisfies two hungers simultaneously; the sexual hunger of the older man and the real hunger of the boy he feeds. (This pederasty/hunger nexus will reach its extreme in *Suddenly Last Summer* when the hungry, naked boys Sebastian Venable sexually exploits literally eat him.) In what amounts to a sexual pun underscored by the young cousin's final line in the story— ". . . *the old man choked to death on our hard candy!*"—hard candy represents both hunger of the phallus and of the stomach. But Mr. Krupper, unlike Williams, is also private, anonymous in the audience of a theater, not the public creator of theatrical and cinematic fantasies. Krupper is allowed an anonymity and mystery forbidden his creator whose late autobiographical work fixes on the unknown, still anonymous, private writer/homosexual.

The young cousin's final line speaks to the public misunderstanding of the private act. To the obituary writer, the old man's death was the sentimental extinction of a man with a sweet tooth and a love for westerns. To the child, a hated old man choked on the products of the family business. The real meaning of the death is a secret between the dead Mr. Krupper and the young men who shared his box at the Joy Rio. It is private and mysterious, reinforcing and embodying Williams's little treatise on mystery. Yet we also have the judgment of the narrator, the only reliable witness, who tells us that Krupper's "private character" was "peculiarly low." In making this harsh judgment on his own creation, the narrator both validates Krupper's story by telling it, and colludes with his "straight" reader by judging it harshly.

As the authorial judgment keeps Williams on the side of his reader, so the smokescreen of mystery, created with what Williams calls "obscurity or indirection," allows him to turn Mr. Krupper's death into something both tawdry and beautiful. While acknowledging his reader's possible scruples and prejudices, he manipulates them, luring his reader to see Mr. Krupper's life and death as at least pathetic. Still, Williams allows no space in this story for alternatives to Mr. Krupper's Joy Rio meetings. Homosexual encounters are furtive, impersonal appeasements of hunger. The operative word is "anonymous," matching Krupper's nonexistent public character. It is interesting to note as well that Krupper's partners enjoyed *or* profited from their encounters with him.

The devices Williams uses in "Hard Candy" are much more typical of his plays than of his fiction. One can see a miniversion of the public/private problem in Blanche's monologue about her husband in *A Streetcar Named Desire*. Blanche tells of "coming suddenly into a room that I thought was empty—which wasn't empty, but had two people in it . . . the boy I had married and an older man who had been his friend for years." This extremely discreet picture of Blanche's discovery of her husband's private homosexuality is followed by her public reaction to it on a crowded dance floor: "I saw! I know! You disgust me . . . ," and then by his public act of suicide. Once made public, Alan's homosexuality becomes unbearable for him: he cannot deal with public disapproval.

Suddenly Last Summer weaves an interesting set of variations on the theme of exposure for the homosexual artist. Sebastian Venable has always been a private artist, wishing to be "unknown outside of a small coterie." The privacy of Sebastian's art is a corollary to his sense that his art is his expression of his religious vision; for the rest of his experience, living was enough: "his life was his occupation." Yet that life was to be even more private than his work: "He *dreaded, abhorred!*—false values that come from being publicly known, from fame, from personal—exploitation." But Sebastian's private life became a public matter when his cousin/wife witnessed his death and devouring at the hands of adolescent boys Sebastian had sexually exploited. To protect Sebastian's privacy, his mother will have Sebastian's widow lobotomized.

Homosexuality in *Suddenly Last Summer* is linked with Sebastian's brutal, carnivorous sense of life, but it is also linked with Williams's private sexual proclivities. Sebastian connects sex with appetite:

> Cousin Sebastian said he was famished for blonds, he was fed up with the dark ones and was famished for blonds. . . . [T]hat's how he talked about people, as if they were—items on a menu —.

Donald Spoto argues convincingly for a strong autobiographical element in *Suddenly Last Summer,* nowhere clearer than in this speech. While in Italy in 1948, Williams wrote Donald Windham: "[Prokosch] says that Florence is full of blue-eyed blonds that are very tender hearted and 'not at all mercenary'. We were both getting an appetite for blonds as the Roman gentry are all sort of dusky types." Sebastian's unfeeling sexual exploitation is as much a dramatization of the playwright as is Sebastian's pill-popping and confused sense of private and public personae.

Cat on a Hot Tin Roof, written around the same time as "Hard Candy," is the most vivid dramatic embodiment of Williams's mixed signals regarding homosexuality and his obsession with public exposure. *Cat* takes place in the bedroom once occupied by Jack Straw and Peter Ochello, a room dominated by the large double bed the lovers shared for thirty years. The plantation the ailing Big Daddy now controls, and which is now being fought over by his potential heirs, was inherited from Straw and Ochello.

In ways both financial and sexual, the legacy of these two lovers lies at the heart of the play, and the love of Jack Straw and Peter Ochello stands as a counter to the compromised heterosexual relationships we see played out. Their relationship, the reader is told in the stage directions, *"must have involved a tenderness which was uncommon,"* yet the audience never hears the relationship spoken of in positive terms. Straw and Ochello do not carry the freight of negative stereotypes other Williams homosexuals carry: they are not frail like Blanche duBois's suicidal husband; nor voracious pederasts like Sebastian Venable, the poet-martyr of *Suddenly Last Summer;* nor are they self-hating like Skipper, the other homosexual ghost in *Cat.* Yet, beyond the stage directions, there is no positive language for Straw and Ochello, who become in the action of the play the targets for Brick's homophobic diatribes.

Straw and Ochello's heir was Big Daddy Pollitt, the cigar-smoking, virile patriarch who admits to loving only two things, his "twenty-eight thousand acres of the richest land this side of the Valley Nile!" and his handsome, ex-athlete son, Brick, who has turned into a drunken recluse since the death of his best friend, Skipper. The central scene in the play is a violent confrontation between patriarch and troubled son in which Big Daddy tries to get at the truth of Brick's relationship with Skipper.

Williams's stage direction tells the reader that Big Daddy *"leaves a lot unspoken"* as he tells Brick of his young years as a hobo and of being taken in and given a job by Jack Straw and Peter Ochello. The implication of the stage direction, and other hints Big Daddy gives in the scene, is that homosexual behavior is not alien to Big Daddy, who "knocked around in [his] time." Yet Brick is so terrified of being called "queer" that he cannot listen to what his father is trying to tell him:

BIG DADDY: ... I bummed, I bummed this country till I was—

BRICK: Whose suggestion, who else's suggestion is it?

BIG DADDY: Slept in hobo jungles and railroad Y's and flophouses in all cities before I—

BRICK: Oh, *you* think so, too, you call me your son and a queer. Oh! Maybe that's why you put Maggie and me in this room that was Jack Straw's and Peter Ochello's, in which that pair of old sisters slept in a double bed where both of 'em died!

BIG DADDY: *Now just don't go throwing rocks at—*

The exchange is a brilliant reversal of expectation: the object of suspicion will not listen to expressions of understanding and tolerance, countering them with homophobic ranting. Brick is obsessed, terrified of being called a "queer," and conscious of the irony of being expected to perform sexually in Straw and Ochello's bed. Big Daddy will allow no attacks on Straw and Ochello, but his defense is interrupted by the appearance of Reverend Tooker, "*the living embodiment of the pious, conventional lie*," an interruption that suggests that it is the pious conventional lie that forbids defense of Straw and Ochello. The interruption is Williams's choice: it allows Brick's homophobic discourse to dominate the scene. In addition to "queer[s]" and "old sisters," Brick speaks of "sodomy," "dirty things," "dirty old men," "ducking [*sic*] sissies," "unnatural thing," and "*fairies*." Brick's acceptance of the pious conventional lie is heard in statements which sound like a caricature of the voice of pious respectability: "Big Daddy, you shock me, Big Daddy, you, you—*shock* me! Talkin' so—casually!—about a—thing like that." Yet his stated reason for his shock is not moral, religious, or psychological; it is public opinion: "Don't you know how people *feel* about things like that? How, how *disgusted* they are by things like that?" Homosexuality to Brick is terrifying because it is inevitably public.

Brick's homophobia is part of his sexual/emotional malaise. He is painfully aware that his nonsexual, nominal marriage to Maggie is a far cry from the total relationship the bed signifies. Brick occupies a perilous middle state: he does not love his wife, with whom he claims never to have gotten any closer "than two people just get in bed which is not much closer than two cats on a—fence humping," an echo of Big Daddy's loveless sex with Big Mama and an expression of Brick's inability to combine sex and friendship or love. Yet he is horrified at the thought of a sexual dimension of his friendship with Skipper: "Why can't exceptional friendship, *real, real, deep, deep friendship* between two men be respected as something clean and decent without being thought of as *fairies*."

Ironically, Maggie, Brick's frustrated wife, understands that Brick's friendship with Skipper "was one of those beautiful, ideal things they tell you about in Greek legends, it couldn't be anything else, you being you, and that's what made it so awful, because it was love that never could be carried through to anything satisfying or even talked about plainly." Maggie knows that it is Brick's "ass-aching Puritanism" that puts him in such an unhappy position—that he would be better off if he had the courage to have a complete relationship with Skipper. But Skipper is dead as a result of his own internalized homophobia, and Brick has, as Big Daddy cogently puts it, "dug the grave of [his] friend and kicked him in it!—before you'd face truth with him!"

The bed of Jack Straw and Peter Ochello represents an unstated ideal relationship which seems unattainable for the heterosexual marriages in Williams's play. In positing this ideal, the play is subversive for its time, yet the love of Jack Straw and Peter Ochello never seems a real possibility for homosexuals either. It is, to coin a phrase from Simon Gray's *Butley*, more a figure of speech than a matter of fact, and a rather paradoxical figure of speech at that, since the only positive words used to describe the relationship are silent hints in the stage directions. The only operative terminology for homosexuals the play allows is Brick's homophobic discourse.

Just at the moment that Big Daddy's dialogue with Brick reaches the crucial issue of Brick's relationship with Skipper, Williams offers a lengthy stage direction which echoes the rejoinder found in "Hard Candy":

> The thing they're discussing, timidly and painfully on the side of Big Daddy, fiercely, violently on Brick's side, is the inadmissible thing that Skipper died to disavow between them. The fact that if it existed it had to be disavowed to "keep face" in the world they lived in, may be at the heart of the "mendacity" that Brick drinks to kill his disgust with. It may be the root of his collapse. Or maybe it is only a single manifestation of it, not even the most important. The bird that I hope to catch in the net of this play is not the solution of one man's psychological problem. I'm trying to catch the true quality of experience in a group of people, that cloudy, flickering, evanescent—fiercely charged!—interplay of five human beings in the thundercloud of a common crisis. Some mystery should be left in the revelation of character in a play, just as a great deal of mystery is always left in the revelation of character in life, even in one's own character to himself. This does not absolve the playwright of his duty to observe and probe as clearly and deeply as he *legitimately* can: but it should steer him away from "pat" conclusions, facile definitions which make a play just a play, not a snare for the truth of human experience.

Williams begins this statement with a definite interpretation of Brick's panic that places responsibility on the false values of Brick's world, then hedges his bets by qualifying his interpretation, then moves the focus away from Brick to the problems of five people, and finally dismisses definite interpretations altogether in the name of "mystery." The last sentence of Williams's little treatise thickens the smokescreen: he wants to offer the truth of human experience without facile conclusions or pat definitions. Fair enough. But he seems to worry about such things only when homosexuality rears its problematic head. Of course, his printed warning is not shared by his audience, only his readers, but it allows him to proceed with a scene about homosexuality while denying that that is what he is doing. At the end of his statement, he directs that the scene between Big Daddy and Brick be "*palpable in what is left unspoken.*" His concern for the unspoken dominates this scene, and what is unspoken here and in the rest of the play is the positive force of the love of Jack Straw and Peter Ochello and the unrealized possibility it represents of a nonhomophobic discourse.

Love is not an operative term for the men in *Cat on a Hot Tin Roof.* It is a word used only by Maggie and Big Mama—the men can only wonder, "Wouldn't it be funny if it were true?" Not able to accept the love of women, neither can the men accept the unspoken option of sexual male/male love. Nor can Williams convincingly offer that option. The tenderness Williams sees as the clear side of his vision here exists only in a stage direction: the cloudiness of homosexuality remains an object of terror, not of the act, but of public exposure.

* * *

While elements of homosexuality suffuse many of Williams's major plays, his later post-Stonewall works deal more directly with his attitudes toward homosexuality. He moves from indirection and poetic image to didacticism and thinly veiled autobiography; the problematics of Williams's treatment of homosexuality become clearer, if less dramatically viable.

Small Craft Warnings (1972) establishes a formula Williams will use again in *Vieux Carré* (1977): the antagonism between a homosexual and a heterosexual "stud," and the placement of a troubled homosexual encounter in the context of a chaotic set of heterosexual relationships. In *Small Craft Warnings* the homosexual character, Quentin, is immediately seen as out of place in the Pacific Coast bar in which the play is set, not because of his sexuality, but because of his appearance, which announces him as a stereotypical homosexual out of a 1940s movie: "dressed effetely in a yachting jacket, maroon linen slacks, and silk neck-scarf." His face, "which seems to have been burned thin by a fever that is not of the flesh," makes him a brother to Williams's many aging male beauties, but here the wasting is an outward manifestation of the spiritual dessication which has resulted from Quentin's sexual promiscuity:

> There's a coarseness, a deadening coarseness, in the experience
> of most homosexuals. The experiences are quick, and hard, and
> brutal, and the pattern of them is practically unchanging. Their
> act of love is like the jabbing of a hypodermic needle to which

they're addicted but which is more and more empty of real
interest and surprise. This lack of variation and surprise in their
. . . "love life" . . . [*He smiles harshly*] . . . spreads into other areas
of . . . sensibility.

The result of this emptying is finally the loss of the "capacity for being
surprised," which is the loss of imagination and, potentially, of the possibility
of creation. Quentin speaks of himself here in the language of textbook
homophobic "objectivity."

Quentin is given the profession of screenwriter, and the experiences
he recounts are those of Williams with MGM in the early 1940s. Moreover,
he now writes pornographic movies, candid depictions of sex, even as
Williams's plays have become more simplemindedly and candidly focused
on sexual activity. These autobiographical clues enable the reader to see
Quentin's emotional diminution not merely as the inevitable result of a
pattern of homosexual activity, but as a corollary of Williams's fear of the
draining away of his emotional and imaginative resources that would eventually cripple his writing. He wrote Donald Windham in 1955, the year of
Cat on a Hot Tin Roof:

I think my work is good in exact ratio to the degree of emotional
tension which is released in it. In a sense, writing of this kind
(lyric?) is a losing game, for steadily life takes away from you, bit
by bit, step by step, the quality of fresh involvement, new, startling reactions to experience, the emotional reservoir is only
rarely replenished . . . and most of the time you are just "paying
out", draining off.

The spiritual waning that cripples the artist becomes here the inevitable cyni-
cism of the aging homosexual who is so self-hating that he can have sex only
with boys who are not homosexual, thus emerging as the most articulate and
least interesting older member of the typical Williams gay liaison: an older
homosexual hungry for the flesh of beautiful, young, heterosexual men.

Williams felt that Quentin's monologue is "much the most effective
piece of writing in the play," and one does see in it an effective duality.
Quentin is suffering the physical and spiritual ravages of time and mortality,
the great nemeses in Williams's world. Yet he also suffers for his awareness
of the brutality of his sex life. The attraction of youth is the attraction of what
has been lost emotionally, and the attraction to heterosexuality is to the
possibility of an alternative to the "coarseness" of homosexual activity. Part
of that coarseness involves the need to keep sex on a financial basis, a matter
of distancing and control which Williams well understood—even his beloved

Frank Merlo was on the payroll. (Williams saw the male prostitute, homo- or heterosexual, as saintly.) Leona tells Bobby, the boy Quentin has picked up, to take Quentin's payment: "He wants to pay you, it's part of his sad routine. It's like doing penance . . . penitence."

Quentin's expression of the homeless place of homosexuality as one cause for his sexual/spiritual malaise is reinforced by echoes from the other characters, who present an image of homosexuality Jerry Falwell would cheerfully endorse. The exuberant, sexually active Leona, tells Quentin:

> I know the gay scene and I know the language of it and I know how full it is of sickness and sadness; it's so full of sadness and sickness, I could almost be glad that my little brother died before he had time to be infected with all that sadness and sickness in the heart of a gay boy.

And Bill, the stud who lives by his cocksmanship with women, who proves himself through fag-bashing—"Y' can't insult 'em, there's no way to bring 'em down except to beat 'em and roll 'em"—at least sees homosexuals as victims of determinism: "They can't help the way they are. Who can?" And Monk, the bartender, does not want gay men in his bar, because eventually they come in droves: "First thing you know you're operating what they call a gay bar and it sounds like a bird cage, they're standing three deep at the bar and lining up at the men's room."

Williams, who did not want to "deal with the didactic, ever," has written here not the gay play he swore he didn't want to write, but a viru-lently homophobic play. The only positive possibility for homosexual expe-rience resides with Bobby, the young man who accompanies Quentin into the bar. Bobby, Williams's typical fantasy youth, is omnisexual, able temporarily to equate sex with love and enjoy whatever experience comes his way. Bobby has the sense of wonder Quentin has lost, a function of youth; all he lacks is the sexual specialization he calls Quentin's "hangup."

Williams's relationship to *Small Craft Warnings* was complex. He saw it, in characteristically dualistic fashion, as "a sort of lyric appeal to my remnant of life to somehow redeem and save me—not from life's end, which can't be revealed through any court of appeals, but from a sinking into shadow and eclipse of everything that had made my life meaningful to me." The play was originally titled "Confessional," which suggests a very personal relationship to the creation. And Williams, to keep the play running long enough to prove that he was still bankable, appeared as Doc through the last weeks of the show's run, though, as Donald Spoto points out, his drunken and drugged shenanigans and foolish ad libs "advertis[ed] the very condition

for which he dreaded condemnation." Ironically, Williams's performances in
Small Craft Warnings were taking place at the same time as his creation of his
most antic public performance, his *Memoirs*, in which the tables are turned
and the public homosexual totally overshadows the private playwright.

Not ironically, but perhaps predictably, the equally confessional *Vieux
Carré* is a desperate mining of memory and early fiction ("The Angel in the
Alcove" [1943]) for material. As with Williams's first success, *The Glass
Menagerie*, this late work is narrated by the playwright as a young man, here
nameless and, alas, faceless. The time is the late thirties, when Williams
finally had his first homosexual experiences, and the setting is a boarding
house in the Vieux Carré. While the play seems to present Williams's
"coming out," the liberation is, at best, conditional. *Vieux Carré* is the most
vivid evidence for the consistency of Williams's attitude toward homosexuality: in the 1943 story and the 1977 play, homosexual activities are characterized as "perversions of longing" experienced by the young writer and an
artist who is fatally diseased. Williams once again presents his past life and
his past material in such a way as to expose himself to his audience while
anticipating and affirming their homophobic reaction.

* * *

In his poem "Intimations" Williams states:

> I do not think that I ought to appear in public
> below the shoulders.
>   Below the collar bone
> I am swathed in bandages already.
> I have received no serious wound as yet
> but I am expecting several.
> A slant of light reminds me of iron lances;
> my belly shudders and my loins contract.

While the poem is about mortality, it also suggests Williams's sense of separation from his own physicality and sexuality as well as his confusion of
private and public selves. In "Intimations" only the mind is public: the body,
of which only the belly and loins are specifically mentioned—appetite and
sexuality—are private and already "swathed in bandages" to cover their
disease. This is a regrettably fitting self-image for Williams the homosexual
and for the homosexuality he depicted throughout his career.

DAVID SAVRAN

"By Coming Suddenly into a Room That I Thought Was Empty": Mapping the Closet with Tennessee Williams

FROST: What about things like the homo-
           sexuality and so on, does everybody
           live with that, too?

WILLIAMS: I think that everybody has some
           elements of homosexuality in him,
           even the most heterosexual of us.

FROST: That no one is all man or all
           woman, you mean?

WILLIAMS: Oh, in my experience, no. I don't
           want to be involved in some sort of a
           scandal, but I've covered the waterfront.
           (*Laughter and applause*)
                     —Television interview with
                     Tennessee Williams (1970)

For Tennessee Williams, homosexuality was the site of manifold contradictions. During his most successful years, the late 1940s and '50s, long before he had come out of the closet, his own identity was articulated in the tension between secrecy and disclosure, between the ability to write his sexual desires and practices silently in his short stories and his inability to speak them openly in his works for the stage or the screen. Homosexuality was Williams's

From *Studies in the Literary Imagination* 24, no. 2 (Fall 1991). © 1991 by the Department of English, Georgia State University.

more or less open secret, the one he neither advertised nor tried to hide by marrying or masquerading as a heterosexual (like many of his Broadway and Hollywood confreres). When Williams finally came out publicly in 1970, on national television, in an interview on "The David Frost Show"—just six months after the Stonewall riot, the beginning of the modern gay liberation movement—it was with a quip that neatly combines fear of disfavor with delight in startling a coy interrogator: "I don't want to be involved in some sort of a scandal, but I've covered the waterfront." This gaily euphemistic amalgam of obfuscation, candor and pride is so characteristic of Williams's plays of the 1940s and '50s (most of which were also greeted with laughter and applause) and accounts for their position as, I believe, the most progressive and radical documents of the period in their figuration of homosexuality. Gore Vidal may characterize Williams as a self-hating homosexual, and John M. Clum may judge the playwright's work to be unrelentingly, if ambiguously, homophobic, but I contend that Williams's work subtly yet powerfully resists the post-War ideological tide. I hope to demonstrate in this essay that, when considered in its historical context, *Cat on a Hot Tin Roof* (1955) dramatizes an almost astonishingly bold rejoinder to the violently homophobic discourses and social practices that prevailed during the so-called domestic revival of the 1950s.

Even a cursory glance at Williams's *Memoirs* and interviews reveals that he conceives his homosexuality in extremely conflicted ways, as a locus of desire and scandal, "freedom" and "crime." Insistently, he renders it both natural and unnatural, allowing it, in Harold Beaver's words, "the dual distinction (and penalty) of simultaneously contravening both 'nature' and 'culture,' fertility and the law." In his many post-Stonewall texts, he provides a deeply equivocal portrait of himself as a homosexual: he is the former "sissy" who later disdains the "'obvious' types" and believes that "travesties of the Mae West . . . make the whole homosexual thing seem ridiculous." He is the one who, harboring "some quite dreadful or abominable secret," was "mortified" at its public revelation, yet who steadfastly maintains that he was "not . . . ever embarrassed particularly by it." He is the one for whom "sex is so much an integral part" of his work that he must continually "talk about it," but who (at least until 1976) never considered it "pertinent to the value of his work" nor found it "necessary" to write "a gay play." He is the one who considers "Gay Lib" a "serious crusade," who insists that all "gay people" should support "legitimate revolutionary movements," who urges the consolidation of "the gay lib movement" with other, "revolutionary" and "nonviolent" organizations, and yet who also maintains that he is "bored" with "movements" and that he finds the "gay libs' public displays . . . so vulgar they defeat their purpose." And he is the one who so delights in these inconsistencies: "I *am* contradictory, baby."

Throughout Williams's work, his homosexuality is both ubiquitous and elusive. It structures and informs all of his texts, yet rarely, especially in his plays, produces the (un)equivocally homosexual character that most critics look for in attempting to identify a homosexual text. Instead, Williams's homosexuality is endlessly refracted in his work: translated, reflected and transposed. Williams insisted, with some justification, that he could not stage his homosexuality directly or candidly during the 1940s and '50s, believing that "there would be no producer for it" given the homophobic program of the Broadway theatre. As a result, he developed a style with distinct similarities to that of his ideological and spiritual forebear, Hart Crane ("a tremendous yet fragile artist"), whose work is analyzed admirably by Thomas E. Yingling in his important new book, *Hart Crane and the Homosexual Text.* Like Crane, Williams wrote (to borrow Yingling's phrase) "under a number of screens and covers" which would allow him to represent his homosexuality in other guises: as a valorization of eroticism generally and extra-marital desire, in particular; as an endorsement of transgressive liaisons that cut across lines of social class, ethnicity and race, and violate mid-century social prescriptions; and as a deep sympathy for the outside and the disenfranchised, for "the fugitive kind."

In the course of Williams's career, the "screens and covers" were constantly redefined and repositioned as a result both of changes in the public profile of the gay writer and of the different visibilities accorded the different media he used. Although several of his short stories from the 1940s and '50s are avowedly and almost jubilantly gay, like "Two on a Party" (1951/52, published 1954), his pre-Stonewall plays and films, written for a much larger and more popular audience, are more cautious and, to use Williams's word, "oblique." In their obliqueness, they embody the unresolved tension between Williams's assertions that he "never tried to disguise [his] homosexuality" and that he "never found it necessary to deal with [homosexuality] in [his] work." Colonizing the contradictory ground between "never tried to disguise" and "never found it necessary to deal," Tennessee Williams consistently writes his homosexuality as equivo-cally as he writes himself in a corpus of work in which "every word is auto-biographical and no word is autobiographical." Throughout his work for the theatre of the 1940s and '50s, homosexuality appears (ever obliquely) as a distinctive and elusive style, in every word and no word, as a play of signs and images, of text and subtext, of metaphorical elaboration and substitu-tion, of disclosure and concealment. It is the open secret that forces even Williams's most homophobic critics to disguise their attacks, upbraiding the playwright, in one carefully coded review, for his "obsessiveness of atti-tude," his "empurpling theatricalism," and his preoccupation with the "sordid," the "lurid" and the "lopsided."

* * *

Tennessee Williams's most productive years, the 1940s and '50s, were extremely turbulent and trying decades for gay men and lesbians in America. Although the '20s and '30s had witnessed the growth of a gay and lesbian subculture in several major cities in the United States, the legal and ideological prohibitions were so stringent that an antihomophobic discursive counterpart was virtually inconceivable. In 1934 the Hollywood production code banned all representations of homosexuality in films. And as John D'Emilio notes, the proscription of homosexual works by the National Office for Decent Literature of the Catholic Church impelled "publishers and newspaper editors" to practice "a form of self-censorship that kept homosexuality virtually out of print." The massive social and demographic disruptions of World War II, meanwhile, allowed a greater possibility for sexual (but not written) expression by gay men and lesbians, both in and out of uniform. Although homosexuals remained officially banned from the military, Alan Berube estimates that "possibly a million or more gay men" were accepted into the armed forces during the War. Gay and lesbian bars may have flourished in the large cities for military and non-military personnel, but this expansion of the gay subculture was accompanied by neither the development of a counter-hegemonic discourse nor the concerted (and, in Jeffrey Weeks's estimation, revolutionary) goal of "personal and sexual self-determination."

When the War ended, gay men and lesbians were once again harassed and subjected—and even more brutally than they had been before—to "witch hunts, bar raids, arrests," which for many encouraged their "retreat to the closet." The late 1940s and '50s were particularly trying, as the House Committee on Un-American Activities pursued a campaign against homosexuals almost as vigorously as they did their crusade against alleged Communist "subversives." According to Senator Joseph McCarthy and his confederates, not only had Hollywood been invaded by Communists, but the very government and the armed forces of the United States had been infiltrated by homosexuals whose presence, they insisted, posed grave security risks. According to the 1950 Republican National Chairman, ninety-one employees of the State Department had been unmasked as "sexual perverts" and summarily fired, in the belief that they were excessively prone to blackmail. During this same period, the job-seekers who were refused Government service and the military personnel who were dismissed as "undesirables" numbered in the thousands. The procedure used to purge the military was particularly insidious because, as D'Emilio notes, "defendants lacked the right to question or even to meet their accusers, and they had no access to the sources used against them." By the end of the 1950s, the anti-homosexual campaign had spread far beyond the government and military. Fanatical vice squads arrested countless men and women in gay and lesbian bars, cruising areas and even their homes, while local newspapers printed the names and addresses of these "perverts," most notoriously in Boise, Idaho. In 1958, a Florida legislator even succeeded in dismissing sixteen faculty and staff members from the State University in Gainesville on charges of homosexuality.

For the first time in the United States, however, a crusade against homosexuals did not proceed unopposed. For this period of intense persecution also marks the beginning of the modern homosexual rights movement, with the founding of the Mattachine Society in 1951 by Henry Hay, a former union organizer and political activist. From its inception, the Society was dedicated to dispelling "the fears and antagonisms of the community," to lobbying for "progressive sexual legislation," and to making "common cause with other minorities in contributing to the reform of judicial, police and penal practices." During the early 1950s, the Society, comprised of gay men and lesbians from across the political spectrum, established chapters in Los Angeles and the San Francisco Bay area. In January 1953, several members of the Society launched *ONE*, a magazine devoted to examining "homosexuality from the scientific, historical and critical point of view." For the remainder of the decade, *ONE* provided a source of information for so-called "homophiles," publishing news of government and police harassment, essays by psychiatrists and sociologists, fiction and reviews of reputedly gay fiction (including Tennessee Williams's book of short stories, *One Arm* [1948; reprinted 1954], which was greeted tepidly). Although its staff included both men and women, most of its contents were clearly addressed to its male readers, whose "problems" and "neuroses" (two obsessively recurring terms) are almost invariably the subject of its feature articles. Its lesbian readers, meanwhile, were saluted dubiously with a column buried in *ONE*'s final pages entitled "The Feminine Viewpoint."

Given both the minuscule dimensions and the relative non-aggressivity of the homosexual rights movement in the early 1950s, and given the limited circulation of *ONE* and other, even smaller magazines for gay men and lesbians, it is especially telling that the forces of political reaction aimed their repressive artillery so determinedly on homosexuals. Zealots like Senator McCarthy and Senator Kenneth Wherry, the Republican floor leader, insisted that there was an indispensable link between Communists and homosexuals, both of whom, in Wherry's estimation, were men "of low morality" and menaces to the American government. Throughout the 1950s, these charges of political subversion were reiterated with a force that too often matched the fury of Senator Wherry, whose "harangues," in columnist Max Lerner's words, were "so violent as to make me think he would explode." This explosive anger was, however, extremely productive for the post-War hegemony insofar as it allowed the principle of containment, which was then the guiding stratagem of American foreign policy, to be exercised on the domestic front. Homophobic panic authorized an unprecedented level of surveillance of social and sexual practices and of political organizations, all in the name of safeguarding the American family and the American way. Even more effectively than allegations of a Communist insurgency, a hunt for homosexuals empowered Congress to police the most private corners of persons' lives and "to regain social control in a world tending towards disorder. . . ."

Despite the radical pasts of Henry Hay and some of the readers of *ONE*, the contents of the magazine exemplify an oddly contradictory collection of texts in which the "homophile" is represented as conflicted and embattled, more an object of social proscriptions than a site of active resistance. The magazine's very statement of purpose betrays an equivocal attitude, on the one hand, announcing its dedication to "educational programs, lectures and concerts," and on the other, drawing attention to the "problems of variation" and calling for "the integration into society of such persons whose behavior and inclinations vary from current moral and social standards." Rather than represent homosexuality as a positivity or call for a radical reconfiguration of the social body, most of the writers for *ONE* speak the language of *remorse*, eschewing revolutionary rhetoric in favor of a guilty appeal for tolerance from the heterosexual majority and for the liberalization of oppressive restrictions. (Hay noted in later years that the Society, at least from 1953 until 1969, was dominated by the doctrine that "All we want to do is to have a little law changed, and otherwise we are exactly the same as everybody else, except in bed.")

What is most striking about the editorial content of *ONE* during the 1950s is the difficulty in distinguishing between a residual discourse of homophobia, with its roots in the "sexology" of the late nineteenth century, and an emergent discourse of gay resistance and liberation which did not really begin to thrive until the mid 1960s. Rather than forge a language in which a newly defined, or even provisionally liberated, homosexual subject could be articulated, *ONE* tended to appropriate the vocabulary (while merely adjusting the attitude) of those mid-century sociological and psychological texts in which homosexual behavior was characterized, in a series of negative definitions, as deviant and neurotic, and the homosexual subject, as incomplete, regressive and guilty.

Like the official texts of the burgeoning homosexual rights movement, most American plays of the 1940s and '50s, even those considered at the time sympathetic to the "problem" of homosexuality, were written in the language of remorse. For the New York theatre, like Hollywood, was subject to strict legislative censorship that worked in complicity with the severe ideological constraints of the period. Dating back to the passage of the so-called Wales Padlock Law in 1927, plays which "depict[ed] or deal[t] with, the subject of sex degeneracy, or sex perversion" were prohibited from the New York stage. During the first post-War years, the theatre practiced a notable self-discipline, faithfully administering this repressive legislation by the homophobic dictates of Lee Shubert, who directed the Shubert monopoly until his death in 1954, and by the eager collusion of the press, particularly the Hearst newspapers.

Although intended as "the first sympathetic dramatic consideration of the homosexual's predicament," Ruth and Augustus Goetz's free adaptation of Andre Gide's *The Immoralist* (1954) recycles the shopworn homophobic conventions. Homosexuality is still the crime that dares not speak its name. The play never uses the word "homosexual" and characterizes the protagonist's "sin of the flesh" as a vile and infectious condition endemic not to the cultivated Europeans but to the "lying and deceitful and bad" Arabs who are promiscuous and dangerous, "like farm animals." The play ends with the protagonist's flight from Algeria and its Orientalist peril and his retreat back into the closet:

> there is no place on earth where those who are like me will not seek me out. Only here in this house where I was raised, can I shut them out.

The most popular play of the 1950s to focus on homosexuality, Robert Anderson's *Tea and Sympathy* (1953), registers a more conflicted, if sympathetic view of its subject than *The Immoralist*. It is a deeply confused work (and, as a result, much more instructive), inveighing against homosexuality, yet plainly revealing the glaring contradictions that inhere within a homophobic, masculinist ideology. With a startling clarity, it dramatizes the extraordinary level of anxiety (and emotional disarray) that coalesces around the constitution of the male homosocial bond, which Anderson characterizes as both a shield against and a symptom of homosexual desire. As is so frequently the case with popular treatments of "social problems," the ending of the play does not attempt to resolve this contradiction, but buries it in a flurry of heterosexual passion and sentiment.

Only in the context of *The Immoralist*, *Tea and Sympathy* and the editorial policy of *ONE*, can one begin to understand the politics of Tennessee Williams's work of the 1940s and '50s and the extent to which his writing mocks his own later insistence that an artist's "politics" and "sexual predilections or deviations are not usually pertinent to the value of his work." I believe that his plays offer far more than the minor adjustment to the rhetoric of homophobia tentatively negotiated by the work of most of his contemporaries. By undermining conventionalized presentations of sexuality and gender, by reconfiguring bourgeois subjectivity *tout court*, and by impugning the sovereignty of theatrical naturalism, they offer a radical—if incompletely realized—challenge to the homophobic fury of the post-War hegemony.

* * *

> The bird that I hope to catch in the net of this play is not the solution of one man's psychological problem. I'm trying to catch the true quality of experience in a group of people, that cloudy, flickering, evanescent—fiercely charged!—interplay of live human beings in the thundercloud of a common crisis.
> —*Cat on a Hot Tin Roof* (1955), Act Two stage directions

Among Williams's most popular and widely esteemed plays, *Cat on a Hot Tin Roof* is the only one to focus on questions of male homosexual desire. In its unusually faithful adherence (for Williams, at least) to the conventions of the well-made play, it carefully manipulates the release of withheld information, and produces an array of secrets—among them, the quintessential "guilty secret" of the 1950s. What appears as the originary event, the possibly homosexual relationship between Brick and Skipper, is barely concealed at all, since most of the characters know most of the story. Furthermore, as is so characteristic of Williams, the exact nature of this open secret is never completely disclosed nor the intrigue that it spawns, resolved. Brick's relationship with his friend, Maggie's (nearly) adulterous liaison with Skipper, and the erotic connections of Big Daddy's youth remain, to some extent, shrouded in the "mystery" that, Williams avers in a stage direction, "should be left in the revelation of character." As a result, a single event in the past is granted neither the legibility nor the fatalistic power with which a playwright like Ibsen or Miller usually endows it.

Despite Williams's near-abandonment of a deterministic form, however, he places particular stress on the dynamics of inheritance. Like *The Cherry Orchard* (1904), *Cat on a Hot Tin Roof* focuses on the death throes of an old regime and dramatizes the conflict between two generations and two social classes for the ownership of a rich estate. The very setting of the play foregrounds the question of inheritance by commemorating the birth of the plantation: the bed-sitting-room once occupied by "a pair of old bachelors," Jack Straw and Peter Ochello, and "haunted" by the "tenderness" they shared, "which was uncommon." When Big Daddy inherited the estate from them, he turned it into "th' biggest an' finest plantation in the Delta," the booty for which the dying patriarch's progeny are now competing. Yet what is most striking about this pattern of estate ownership is less its conspicuously patrilineal nature, than the homosexuality that stands at its imputed origin and so determinedly "haunts" its development. For not only has Big Daddy inherited the plantation from Straw and Ochello, but he has also inadvertently passed along at least a glimmer of homosexual desire to his younger son, Brick, a man driven to despair (and alcohol) over the death of his friend Skipper and married to a woman he "can't stand."

Structurally, Big Daddy functions as the carrier of homosexuality—the heir to the estate, engineered "by hook or crook," and the man who confesses to having "knocked around in [his] time." But Big Daddy is paying a terrible price for his youthful prodigality (a price that would not be out of line in *The Immoralist*). He is dying of bowel cancer, which, as in Williams's short story, "The Mysteries of the Joy Rio" (1941; published 1954), becomes the currency of mortal debt in Williams's homosexual economy, the transcendent commodity, which (along with capital and real estate) is passed from the homosexual progenitor to his progeny. For Big Daddy, bowel cancer seems to be the wages of sodomy (or at least, of "knock[ing] around"). In contrast, his own heir, Brick, must suffer self-hatred, a less life-threatening reward for a less tangible crime: the experience of (or incitement of another to) homosexual desire.

In *Cat on a Hot Tin Roof*, however, homosexuality is not only destructive and cancerous. For Williams's most original move in the play is to turn Big Daddy, despite—or perhaps because of—the taint of homosexuality, into the play's exemplum of normative masculinity. In the words of Arthur Miller, who has a particularly keen eye for such things, Big Daddy is "the every image of power, of materiality, of authority," the very model of a promiscuous—and misogynist—heterosexuality. With his "lech" for Maggie and his deathbed longing for a young, "choice" mistress, his contempt for Big Mama's "fat old body," for her "sound" and "smell," yet his dutiful service to her ("*laid* her . . . regular as a piston"), he seems to epitomize the orthodox heterosexual masculinity of the 1950s that simultaneously desires and degrades women.

Yet unlike the most popular icons of masculinity during the 1950s, Williams's male subjects are sites of division, instability and contradiction. Homosexual desire is cast not as masculinity's anathema but as that which always already inheres inside the male subject (like a cancer). Homosexuality and homosociality are no longer represented as unmediated opposites, but as fluid and complicitous states of desire. To represent these desires, Williams engineers a kind of trade off around questions of (internalized) homophobia, whose symptoms are displaced from the attitudinal to the medical. By inscribing Big Daddy's viscera with the signs of a malignant homophobia, Williams is able to provide him ideologically with this cancer's benign opposite: an antihomophobic position from which to preach "*tolerance!*" Furthermore, this ideological position also permits him to be exceptionally sensitive to economic injustice, whether to the plight of naked Spanish children "beggin' like starvin' dogs with howls and screeches," or to the child prostitutes of Marrakech. In the same gesture, it endows him with a remarkable understanding of the implacable logic of the commodity that decrees that "the human animal . . . buys and buys and buys" in its attempt to fend off death, hoping against hope that "one of [its] purchases will be life everlasting!" More clearly than any other character's, Big Daddy's desires illuminate the symmetry that runs throughout Williams's work between the commodity (that attracts yet never satisfies) and the commodified status of homosexuality (that attracts and repels with a dismally lurid radiance).

Yet *Cat on a Hot Tin Roof* is, I believe, even more radical than Big Daddy's divided subject position would suggest. For the analysis of character and action performed above assumes a measure of comprehensibility and of unity to both which, I believe, the play subtly yet assiduously belies. The more closely one examines the construction of subjectivity in *Cat on a Hot Tin Roof*, the less securely it seems to conform to the orthodox patterns dictated by the well-made play or the liberal sociology of the 1950s. The more closely one examines the printed text (either the original or the Broadway version), the more eccentric it seems, its exorbitant stage directions swarming with philosophical reflections, almost microscopically specific character descriptions, and vividly pictorial metaphors.

The practice of writing extensive stage directions in dramatic texts dates from the mid-nineteenth century and parallels the development of Realism. From Ibsen to Shaw to Miller, the realistic playwright uses stage directions in an attempt to consolidate his or her almost monopolistic control over the interpretation of the printed text in the face of several challenges to the authorial prerogative: the modern stage director, the development of competing styles of acting and scenic design, and the gradual elimination of lines of business. In addition to providing pointers to characterization and markers of subtext for actor and director, however, stage directions also serve as a guide for the nonprofessional reader, as a device to link a series of discrete speech acts into an apparently seamless movement. In most Realistic plays, these supplementary—that is, absolutely crucial—jottings play a key role in constituting the dramatic characters as coherent subjects for whom the gap between spoken and unspoken, or action and desire, can be analyzed according to (various) psychological principles and thereby successfully negotiated. By producing ostensibly whole characters and an almost novelistic sense of continuity, they carefully regulate the operation of empathic identification and, as a result, play a vital role in supervising the reader's interpellation in the text.

Although Williams often uses stage directions in the manner of the orthodox Realist, his texts also allow these authorial interjections to perform a very different function. Tellingly, it is not a patently surrealistic play like *Camino Real* (1953) that most challenges their traditional use, but Williams at (in his own words) his "most realistic," in *Cat on a Hot Tin Roof.* The elaborate stage directions in that play provide perhaps the most revealing example of Williams's practice of fracturing the coherence of both the Realistic text and the ostensibly stable subject that takes up residence within it. From the very beginning of the play, the private interactions of Maggie and Brick (in Act One) and Brick and Big Daddy (in Act Two) are almost continually invaded or interrupted by the various comings and goings, the screaming, songs and laughter of Big Mama, Mae, Gooper and the "no-neck monsters." With anarchic precision, these private scenes are broken by wildly incongruous sonic disruptions, by the "children shriek[ing] downstairs," by their "loud but uncertain" singing, by a child "burst[ing] into the room . . . firing a cap pistol . . . and shouting: 'Bang, bang, bang!'" by the "blast . . ." of "a Wagnerian opera or a Beethoven Symphony," by a "hideous bawling," by a "scat song," and finally by Big Daddy's off-stage wail, his "long drawn cry of agony and rage."

These interruptions (that are predictably quieted and softened by those directors for whom Williams is merely a slightly queer Realist) work in complex ways not only to fracture dramatic continuity but also to decenter the scenic representation. The force and violence of these intrusions and noises from elsewhere create the impression that the scenes enacted on stage, despite their dramatic urgency, are just a tiny part of a much more extensive and extravagant series of actions that constantly exceeds the bounds of theatrical representation. One way of conceptualizing the room represented on stage, the bed-sitting-room of Jack Straw and Peter Ochello, is as a modern analog to what Roland Barthes calls the Racinian Antechamber: a space between, a room in which one waits, a "site of language," of debate, that stands in opposition to the turbulence outside. It is at once a refuge from the world and from action, a private, indeed, erotic chamber, and yet one whose privacy is always being violated, and whose inhabitants are constantly being monitored by curious and greedy persons looking for an opportunity to bring disgrace and ruin upon them. When described in this way, however, the bed-sitting-room seems less a neo-classical preserve than the space of the *closet*, of the open secret, the chamber in which the reign of (homosexual) patriarchy was conceived and delivered, and over which an almost constant surveillance is posted, with spies always lurking just outside its closed doors or always attempting to eavesdrop through its fragile walls. It is a permeable space, only minimally distinct from the upstairs gallery that borders it and lies just beyond its "two pairs of very wide doors," containing a bathroom whose contents are barely discernable to the audience. It is dominated by two pieces of furniture, a "big double bed which staging should make a functional part of the set as often as suitable," and a "monumental monstrosity peculiar to our times, a *huge* console" containing radio-phonograph, television and liquor cabinet. According to the stage directions, this console is itself a kind of miniature closet, or a closet-within, "a very complete and compact little shrine to virtually all the comforts and illusions behind which we hide. . . ."

Throughout Williams's work, the closet (this "monumental monstrosity peculiar to our times") is the subject of innumerable metaphoric and metonymic transformations, a constantly shifting site of concealment and disclosure, speech and silence. In *Cat on a Hot Tin Roof*, it is represented by the bed-sitting-room; in *The Glass Menagerie* (1944), by the movie theatre to which Tom makes a nightly pilgrimage; in *A Street-car Named Desire* (1947), by that chamber that Blanche discovers inadvertently "By coming suddenly into a room that I thought was empty—which wasn't empty, but had two people in it. . . ." It is a place of darkness and violence, a place whose mysterious geography and proscribed contents are articulated by the almost surrealistic juxtaposition of the verbal and the visual, by the strangely under-stated lucidity of Blanche's diction (figuratively) colliding with "*the headlight*" of a locomotive that, immediately after Blanche's revelation, suddenly "*glares into the room as it thunders past.*" It is a fantasmic site that is crucial for the definition of private space and private persons in a homophobic culture, "centrally representative," in Eve Sedgwick's words, of the culture's "moti-vating passions and contradictions, even while marginalized by its ortho-doxies." It is the primal scene of Williams's drama, the culturally (rather than solitarily) produced central core usually relegated to an off-stage position, the empty/not empty room in which the homosexual subject is constructed.

In *Cat on a Hot Tin Roof* the constitution of the subjects that inhabit Williams's closet/bed-sitting-room is even more startling than the latter's geography and permeability. As Eve Sedgwick notes, "in this century . . . homosexual definition . . . is organized around a radical and irreducible incoherence." Throughout the play, this incoherence is encoded not only in the relative instability of both male and female subject positions—Maggie is not the only character who scampers and bounds through the action like a cat on a hot tin roof—but also in the way that the text (especially its voluminous stage directions) figures forth the bodies of the *dramatis personae*. Insistently, Williams destabilizes and ruptures the coherence of the self-identical subject, turning all of the characters into subhuman creatures or else human beings so radically fragmented, diseased or wounded as to be barely recognizable as human. The more peripheral, greedy and hateful figures are transformed into animalistic grotesques. They range from the "no-neck monsters" with "dawgs' names" to the hissing and grimacing Mae to the more sympathetic, yet strangely protean Big Mama, whose dress bears "large irregular patterns" resembling "the markings of some massive animal," and whose "fat old body" alternates in appearance between that of an "old bulldog" and a "charging rhino."

The three principals are not, however, decisively contrasted (as unified subjects) with these embodiments of a gross and literally inhuman materialism. Like his wife, Big Daddy is constructed as a large animal who "wheezes and pants and sniffs" and who is, of course, being destroyed from within by cancer. The incarnation of patriarchal and material authority, his body stages the contradictions inherent in the commodity: the impossible intersection of desire and disgust, of homosexual and heterosexual generation, of misogynist and antihomophobic discourse, and of his struggle against the social uremia that results from "the failure of the body to eliminate its poisons." Brick, meanwhile, is fashioned with a similar physical disequilibrium. He is an alcoholic who is "still slim and firm as a boy" only because "his liquor hasn't started tearing him down outside." He is a man who is physically crippled, whose ankle "is broken, plastered and bound," and yet who retains the aloof air of a "godlike being." Of the three, Maggie, a "pretty young woman," is the most subtly and yet the most radically fragmented, produced discursively as a collection of disarticulated corporeal details, an assemblage of body parts, a strange construction that "*giggles with a hand fluttering at her throat and her breast and her long throat arched.*" Throughout Act One, Williams's stage directions teem with Maggie's parts: arms, armpits, eyelash; hand, throat, breast; fist, mouth; head, brows; shoulders, arms, fists, eyes, head, throat—with never a whole body in sight.

This peculiar fragmentation is the result, I believe, of Maggie's status as the play's primary desiring subject, the one "consumed with envy an' eaten up with longing," not only for Brick, but also for the "beautiful, ideal . . . noble" and "clean" relationship between Brick and Skipper from which she feels utterly excluded. When she attempts to force her way into this relationship (that decisively unsettles the distinction between homosocial and homosexual desire), making love to Skipper, it is because, "it made both of us feel a little bit closer to [Brick]," the common object of desire. Since her liaison with Skipper, Brick's repudiation of him, and Skipper's quasi-suicide, Maggie has become the inheritor, the mediator in a now-immobilized erotic triangle between the living and the dead, the woman who desires to be a partner in an impossible and belated erotic fascination, the woman who, in coveting Brick's aloofness, desires his very refusal to desire her. Likewise, in Brick's imagination, Maggies takes up a similarly contradictory position, representing both obstacle and goal, both the barrier to the fulfillment of his desire and the symbolic repository of Skipper's own sexuality. It is perhaps as the latter, as the locus of an impossible and proscribed desire, that Maggie's body comes into focus as being not only commodified and fragmented, but fetishized. Like the "no-neck monsters" she vilifies in the very first line of the play, she is constituted distinctively by the body part she lacks. In the case of her young in-laws, the absence of necks epitomizes their monstrosity. In her case, however, the absent phallus becomes reinscribed in her body and so allows her to be produced as an object of desire. In her Act One narrative, her liaison with Skipper—in which he proved impotent—is figured as a ritual of castration, the appropriation (or theft) of the other's phallus that reimprints it metonymically in every limb and recess of her body, so turning her into an object of erotic fascination for the writer of the stage directions, if not for Brick.

Maggie's status as a fetishized object, a phallic woman, the sign of both erotic desire and castration, is not, however, simply a benign transfiguration of this "pretty young woman." Rather, she becomes the play's prime example of what Lacan designates as the "imagos of the fragmented body," the images of "castration, mutilation, dismemberment, dislocation, evisceration, devouring, bursting open of the body" which "represent the elective vectors of aggressive intentions." Although, throughout *Cat on a Hot Tin Roof*, these aggressive intentions are aimed in many different directions, at many different subjects (producing both Big Daddy's cancer and Brick's broken ankle), they are directed with particular (because almost subliminal) violence against women. They motivate Brick's brutal swipe at Maggie with his crutch that "shatters the gemlike lamp on the table," and seem to provoke Big Daddy's vicious threat to Mae: "I'll have your bones pulverized for fertilizer!"

Yet *Cat on a Hot Tin Roof*'s configuration of a female body constantly in danger of disintegrating does not mean that the male body is constructed as its opposite. Insistently, the male body is as fragmented (if in a different way) as its female counterpart. Like his wife, Brick is rendered a fetishistic object, his distinctive status marked by the elongated white sheath wrapped around his leg, his cast, rather than, like Maggie, by the dismembering yet silent violence of the stage directions. Like the eponymous hustler, murderer and ex-boxer of the story, "One Arm", (written 1942–45; published 1948), whose absent limb commemorates his desirability—and his abjection—Brick's plastered leg is the sign of his status as a commodity, as an object of devotion, as a castrated man (more object than subject of desire, neither fully hetero- nor homosexual) whose phallus is silently and, in this case, metaphorically reinscribed elsewhere.

The different modes of corporeality in *Cat on a Hot Tin Roof*, the fragmentation of the body or the fetishistic encasement of a limb in plaster, are the visible signs of guilt and eroticism, anxiety and power, confinement and freedom, secrecy and disclosure—in short, all the emotional equivocations that characterize the inhabitants of the closet. In their dual and interdependent figuration as fetishized bodies, Brick and Maggie, the castrated man and the phallic woman, cut diagonally across the culturally produced antitheses between subject and object, masculinity and femininity, homosexuality and heterosexuality, or more exactly, expose the arbitrary and provisional nature of these binarisms. They do so by installing in their place unstable sets of sheer difference that resist being conceptualized as polar opposites: desire and sterility, the phallus and its displacements, metonymy and metaphor, the scenic and the textual, spoken dialogue and (silent) stage directions. In *Cat on a Hot Tin Roof*, as throughout Williams's work, genders and sexualities are not set in opposition but are dispersed and plural, constantly in circulation, like the rose tattoo (in the play of the same name), constantly reappearing in unexpected places, on unexpected bodies. The nomadic subjects produced by this process are much like those Williams elsewhere labels "make-shift arrangements," those he describes to Donald Windham during one of his "periodic neuroses," or "blue devils," as he calls them:

> Naturally we have very little integrity, if any at all. Naturally the innermost "I" or "You" is lost in a sea of other disintegrated elements, things that can't fit together and that make an eternal war in our natures. . . . We all bob only momently above the bubbling, boiling surface of the torrent of lies and distortion we are borne along.

In *Cat on a Hot Tin Roof*, Williams radically redefines both the self and the other, the "I" and the "You" that is "lost in a sea" of "disintegrated elements," and cunningly destabilizes normative constructions of sexuality. This destabilization is rendered particularly vividly by Maggie's final and peripetous confession, her invented pregnancy, which, ironically, becomes a testament not to the "naturalness" of heterosexuality, but to the impossibility of erasing male homosexual desire, and to Skipper's irrevocable position in the erotic triangle. For even if Brick were to accede to Maggie's demand and agree to "make the lie true" (in Maggie's words), he would not resolve the question of his own sexual identity, nor confirm the primacy of heterosexual desire, not an iota of which Brick displays. His successful impregnation of his wife in the bed of Jack Straw and Peter Ochello would ironically attest less to the sudden and timely triumph of a "natural" heterosexuality, than to the perpetuation of a homosexual economy and to the success of Maggie's fetishistic appropriation of Skipper's sexuality. (It is in this sense that Brick's act of making the lie of Maggie's pregnancy true would also make true the "lie" about Brick and Skipper.)

Although *Cat on a Hot Tin Roof* reveals many of the contradictions inscribed in homophobic ideologies and practices, it simultaneously bears witness to the (at times) painfully oblique discourse that must be spoken in and around the closet during the 1950s. It attests distressingly to the level of aggressivity that may be unleased against its occupants: the violence that dismembers, maims, ravages—and eroticizes—the inhabitants of the empty/not empty room. At the same time, the play ironically proves how crucial this site is for the construction of a theory of patrilinearity during the triumphalist display of containment during the 1950s. It demonstrates that the closet, like the "glass box" in which Brick had worked as a sports announcer and from which he had watched the games, is less a means of concealment than a privileged perspective on both the cultural dominant and that which it seeks to police and contain: those very adventures for which Brick is no longer deemed "fit," the tumultuous sexual contests in which men are engrossed in "sweating out their disgust and confusion."

By the end of this widely acclaimed and, indeed, Pulitzer Prize-winning play, Williams begins cautiously to redefine the male homosexual subject, less by conceiving of him as a positivity than as a kind of absent (off-stage) presence—like Skipper, or Jack Straw and Peter Ochello, or the phallus inscribed in Maggie's dismembered body. For in 1955 Williams was able to protect this homosexual subject from "the torrent of lies and distortions" that overwhelms him on the commercial stage only by displacing him, or by not allowing him to speak, since the only language he was permitted to speak was the very one that ensured his abjection and his marginalization. By appropriating the language of convention (and subtly turning it against itself), and by absenting the homosexual subject (and drawing attention to his absence), another homosexual subject, Tennessee Williams, is allowed not only to speak, but virtually to reign over the commercial theatre of the 1940s and '50s. Long before Stonewall, and during a period of brutal and murderous homophobia, Williams's "most realistic" play practices a cautious sleight of hand, simultaneously articulating a potentially revolutionary site of resistance and reducing the discourse of homophobia to a barely comprehensible babble.

CHRISTOPHER BRIAN WEIMER

Journeys from Frustration to Empowerment: Cat on a Hot Tin Roof *and Its Debt to* García Lorca's Yerma

YERMA: Some things don't change! There are things locked up behind the walls that can never change because nobody hears them! . . . But if they suddenly exploded, they would shake the world!

MAGGIE: When something is festering in your memory or your imagination, laws of silence don't work, it's just like shutting a door and locking it on a house on fire in hope of forgetting that the house is burning. But not facing a fire doesn't put it out. Silence about a thing just magnifies it. It grows and festers in silence, becomes malignant.

The extent to which Federico García Lorca's works influenced Tennessee Williams's creative output remains a largely neglected question, one often passed over in favor of Williams's debt to Anton Chekov and D. H. Lawrence. However, Lorca (1899–1936) was one of the authors whom Williams (1911–1983) studied intensively during his college years, while a 1947 *New York Times* interviewer reported that "among his favorite writers are Chekov and the Spanish poet and dramatist García Lorca, and it is prob-

---

From *Modern Drama* 35, no. 4 (December 1992). © 1992 by the University of Toronto.

able that they, more than any others, have contributed to his own particular style." Nowhere is Lorca's influence more apparent than in Williams's early one-act *The Purification*, a rural tragedy in verse clearly modeled after the Spanish author's *Bodas de sangre* (*Blood Wedding*).

A better-known Williams play to which Lorca's contribution has gone previously unexplored is the 1955 *Cat on a Hot Tin Roof*; even a brief consideration of its similarities to Lorca's *Yerma* (1934) will indicate the earlier drama's importance as a source for Williams's Broadway success. Paul Binding describes Lorca's subject in *Yerma* as "frustration in a restricted society," words that would also serve as an apt description of *Cat*'s stifling emotional atmosphere. Each work revolves around a central female figure, a woman whose dilemmas give the drama momentum and whose resolution of those dilemmas brings down the final curtain: Yerma and Maggie the Cat. Like Yerma, Maggie is a faithful woman who yearns for children but is trapped in a childless marriage. Just as Yerma's husband Juan dismisses her maternal desires, Maggie's spouse Brick likewise refuses to accept or act on her feelings. The essential conflict in both plays results from the clash of wills between husband and wife, and each clash is resolved when the woman takes control of her situation through decisive action: Yerma kills Juan, while Maggie blackmails Brick into bed for the express purpose of siring a child. This paper will explore *Cat*'s debt to *Yerma* further and in greater detail, in hopes of illuminating fresh aspects of the later play as well as Williams's creative process.

Extending Binding's description of *Yerma*'s dramatic essence to *Cat on a Hot Tin Roof* would be impossible if the two dramas did not take place in similarly restrictive societies. As Reed Anderson emphasizes, Lorca sought "to represent in his tragic theater the complex interaction between the individual consciousness of his characters and the material and social circumstances of their lives." What, then, are those circumstances? Juan and Yerma are members of the rural peasantry in Andalusia, and Anderson makes it clear that two vital aspects of their tragedy stem from their socioeconomic status: their bondage to the land they own, and their bondage to the rigid honor code along with its demanding set of gender role expectations. Although Juan owns property and should therefore be its master, he is in fact its slave, because only his continual, back-breaking labor persuades it to produce. Yerma tells him, "You work hard, and you aren't strong enough for so much work," just as Juan himself admits his frustration with his toil and his resultant inability to enjoy its fruits. And while Yerma is a supremely faithful wife to Juan, her refusal to sequester herself within his house nevertheless threatens him, because the social conventions of honor consider appearances alone. Although Yerma defends her virtue, declaring, "take care you don't put another man's name on my breast!" Juan replies by invoking public opinion:

> It's not me who puts it there—you put it there with your behavior, and the town is beginning to talk! Beginning to talk! When I join a group of people, they all grow quiet. When I go to weigh the flour, they all grow quiet. And even at night, when I wake up in the fields, it seems as if the branches of the trees grow quiet, too!

We see here rural Andalusia's dual-armed power structure: economic and social. Each arm possesses sufficient weight to warp the spirit of the members of that society, and together they oppress Juan and Yerma to such a degree that their mutual tragedy is inevitable.

The dynamics of *Cat on a Hot Tin Roof* also have their roots in the interaction between Williams's characters and the inescapable socioeconomic forces which they face, in this case those of the American South. Big Daddy Pollitt is far wealthier than Juan; like him, however, Big Daddy's life has been devoted to the productivity of his property, "twenty-eight thousand acres of the richest land this side of the Valley Nile." Further, the greed for control of Big Daddy's holdings after his impending death motivates many of *Cat*'s characters, and it is the question of to whom he should entrust those holdings that frustrates Big Daddy himself. (In addition, the two works share a central irony: both are dramas of human infertility set in subcultures where the question of agricultural fertility is always paramount.) Williams also repeatedly emphasizes the social realities of the American South in *Cat*. References to public opinion and social status are frequent, while gender role expectations are strongly emphasized: Maggie and her sister-in-law Mae, as women, are expected to bear children just as the former football star Brick and his brother Gooper are expected to sire them; it is taken for granted that a male Pollitt must take control of the plantation after Big Daddy's death; last and most vital of all, Brick's moral deterioration and alcoholism both stem from his inability to accept the possibility of a homoerotic element in his friendship with his teammate Skipper. The characters in *Cat* are every bit as much victims of their environment as those in *Yerma*, and those environments are in fact remarkably similar.

Having earlier established the fundamental structural kinship between the two title heroines, I now hope to explore their psychological kinship and make it clear how much Williams's characterization of Maggie owes to Lorca's Yerma. Each is a woman notable for her hunger for motherhood, sensuality, sense of integrity, and unbreakable determination that ultimately gives her the strength necessary for self-empowerment.

Obviously, Yerma's obsessive maternal yearning is central to the play that bears her name. One way Lorca establishes this is by presenting us with Yerma's anguished responses to frequent reminders of her barren state; the most heartbreaking of all is her observation of the resemblance between her neighbor Maria and the latter's child: "He has the same eyes that you have." For Yerma, the bearing of children is her life's purpose, and her failure to do so threatens to invalidate her entire existence: "A woman from the country who doesn't bear children is as useless as a handful of thorns—even sinful!" Julianne Burton points out that Yerma has simply internalized the beliefs of a society that considers a woman's handiwork and children her only wealth, and declares, "Children are the fulfillment and the legitimization of women, which is why Yerma so desperately seeks a child."

Like Yerma, Maggie needs children and is constantly reminded of her failure to produce them, even by her little niece Dixie: "You're *jealous!*— You're just jealous because you can't have babies!" Maggie's desperate desire for offspring, however, is quite different in its fundamental motivation from Yerma's. Her primary need for them is economic: Brick is the favored son of the dying Big Daddy, but his testamentary prospects still depend on his willingness to carry on the family line. Brick, unfortunately for both himself and Maggie, is sunk in nearly total apathy toward everything, and will not lift a finger to interfere with Gooper's plan to seize control of all the Pollitt holdings with the help of his grotesquely fertile wife Mae. Maggie, on the other hand, understands the situation all too well, as she makes clear when she refers to Gooper and Mae's "constant little remarks and innuendos about the fact that you and I have not produced any children, are totally childless and therefore totally useless!" Maggie's reason for desiring motherhood is diametrically opposed to Yerma's, yet her need for maternity's socially ordained legitimacy is identical.

Lorca establishes Yerma's sensual nature during her interrogation by the First Old Woman, when she confesses her physical response to the shepherd Victor in the past:

> Victor . . . took me by the waist, and I couldn't say anything to him because I couldn't talk. Another time, this same Victor—fourteen years old, and big for his age—took me in his arms to help me over a ditch, and I began to tremble so hard my teeth rattled!

However, Yerma represses her sensuality, admitting that she equates sex not with pleasure, but with the siring of children. "For his sake, I gave myself to my husband," she says, referring to her unborn son, "and I keep giving myself to make sure he's on the way—but never for my own pleasure!" Yerma demonstrates her aversion to her own sexuality throughout the play, and Rupert C. Allen even argues that she strangles the unexpectedly concupiscent Juan in the final scene because his "lewdness symbolizes (in the form of a projection) an impulse within herself, which she has repressed throughout the drama."

Williams leaves no doubt that Maggie shares Yerma's intense sensuality. When she tries to arouse Brick with a graphic description of Big Daddy's obvious appreciation of her body, we see a woman completely in tune with her own erotic nature. In addition, however, a vital change which Williams made in his heroine becomes apparent: Maggie revels in her eroticism, without any of Yerma's fears or repressions. Yerma is a woman stifling her own sexuality, while Maggie's is stifled by Brick's refusal to sleep with her. It is this sexual denial that makes Maggie "feel all the time like a cat on a hot tin roof" and makes her refer to her current celibate existence as "the martyrdom of Saint Maggie."

The third primary characteristic shared by Lorca and Williams's eponymous heroines is their strong sense of personal integrity. Neither will compromise herself to the slightest degree, although both are offered opportunities to do so. Yerma, for example, demonstrates her steadfastness with two separate refusals: that of Juan's offer to adopt one of her brother's children, and that of the First Old Woman's offer to take Yerma into her home and provide her son to impregnate Yerma. To accept Juan's offer would mean renouncing any hope of bearing her own offspring, and it is inconceivable that Yerma as we know her would even entertain the idea: "I don't want to take care of other people's children! I think my arms would freeze just holding them!" she tells Juan. Yerma's ideals demand, in the words of Anderson, "her participation in the shared experience of creating and perpetuating human life through bearing children." It is the burning purity of this desire for biological motherhood that helps to define Yerma; she is incapable of settling for anything less. By the same token, Yerma is incapable of accepting the First Old Woman's proposition. When scorning it, she rises to one of her finest moments in the entire drama, a speech in which she defiantly brandishes her own integrity:

> Be quiet, be quiet, it's not that! I'd never do that! I can't go out looking. Do you think that I could have another man? What about my honor? You can't turn back the tide or have a full moon come out at midday! Go away! I'll continue on the road I have chosen. Did you really think that I could turn to another man? That I'm going to beg like a slave for what belongs to me? Understand what I am saying, so that you will never speak to me again! I am not looking for anyone.

Yerma's honor, as Binding emphasizes, "demands that Juan—and Juan only—must be the father of her child." And although maintaining her honor leads inexorably to tragedy, Yerma can do nothing else.

In much the same way, Maggie is true to Brick. Once again, the psychology of the Williams heroine has a different dimension: while Yerma admits that she does not love Juan, Maggie's love for Brick is still passionate although not reciprocated. When Brick actually suggests that Maggie relieve her sexual frustration with another man, she vehemently refuses to cuckold her husband, even with his consent and encouragement; in her own words (words which Yerma might have echoed), she is "not that common." And just as in the case of Yerma, Maggie's maintenance of her honor has cost her a great deal of pain: "*Oh, Brick!* How long does it have t' go on? This punishment? Haven't I done time enough, haven't I served my term, can't I apply for a—pardon?" Nor will Maggie pretend to be anything she is not:

> —I'm not tryin' to whitewash my behavior, Christ, no! Brick, I'm not good. I don't know why people have to pretend to be good, nobody's good. The rich or the well-to-do can afford to respect moral patterns, conventional moral patterns, but I could never afford to, yeah, but—I'm honest! Give me credit for just that, will you *please*?

Williams's heroine differs from Lorca's in her degree of respect for and internalization of conventional morality. But more important, Yerma and Maggie are both obsessively true to their marriage vows and to themselves, no matter what the price for that truth may be.

The final quality with which Williams endows Maggie is Yerma's determination to achieve her desires. Each heroine finds herself in a position from which no victory seems possible, yet neither abandons hope. Despite Juan's clear opposition, not until the final climax of *Yerma* do we see her even consider giving up her quest for children. In the fourth of the drama's six scenes, years after the beginning of the play, this particularly powerful exchange between Yerma and her husband reveals just how inflexible her resolve is:

JUAN: Being around you only makes me restless and uneasy. When there's no other choice, you should resign yourself.

YERMA: I came to this house so I wouldn't have to resign myself! When I'm in my coffin with my hands tied together and a cloth wrapped around my head to keep my mouth from falling open—that's when I'll resign myself!

And when Juan's implacability drives Yerma to what Binding terms "her one deed of triumphant passion"—her husband's murder—Yerma is, paradoxically, a tragic yet victorious figure. As Burton declares, "she feels free and confident at last." She has proved herself stronger than Juan and taken from him the control he exercised over her; whatever now befalls her will be the result of her own actions.

Similarly, Maggie the Cat never has the slightest intention of allowing Gooper and Mae to triumph in the fight for those twenty-eight thousand acres. As she warns Brick in the first act, "But one thing I don't have is the charm of the defeated, my hat is still in the ring, and I am determined to win!" That victory, however, will require a child, and when Brick asks her how she proposes to have one by him when he cannot even stand her, Maggie answers grimly: "That's a problem I will have to work out." Maggie's determination has many roots, among them her refusal to give up on her relationship with Brick and the memory of her grinding poverty prior to marriage. But those roots are ultimately irrelevant; what *is* relevant is her final triumph. In falsely declaring her pregnancy to Big Daddy and then forcing Brick to "make the lie come true," Maggie acts from strength rather than reacting out of weakness, and like Yerma, empowers and frees herself.

Both *Yerma* and *Cat* feature two important male characters: the former, Juan and Victor; the latter, Brick and Big Daddy. At first the plays' similarities in this respect appear to be overwhelmed by their differences, and it seems that Williams's Southern men owe little to their Andalusian counterparts. Juan could not be less like Brick in most ways, there is no Victor-figure in *Cat*, and there is no equivalent of Big Daddy in *Yerma*. However, I believe this to be a superficial judgement. The key lies in examining the dramatic functions served by the men in each play. In *Yerma* Juan is a husband who refuses to fulfill his reproductive responsibilities and a patriarch, in the ideological sense although not the dynastic one, whose wife speaks repeatedly of his physical decline; Victor seems to embody the fertile virility which Juan lacks and toward which Yerma is so drawn. In *Cat*, Big Daddy is another patriarch betrayed by his own failing health, while Brick is both a husband rejecting his conjugal duties and a source of masculine sexual allure. It should now be apparent that Williams has simply redistributed the dramatic functions served by Lorca's two primary male characters. In *Yerma* we see Victor embody a dramatic function that we might label the Virile Youth, while in Juan we see the Sexually Withdrawn Husband and the Ailing Patriarch. In *Cat* Brick embodies both the Virile Youth and the Sexually Withdrawn Husband, with Big Daddy as the Ailing Patriarch.

The function of the Virile Youth scarcely requires explanation. Yerma's intense physical response to Victor has already been cited; also, in the dream interlude that begins the play, Yerma's unborn child is led by a shepherd on tiptoe who stares at Yerma, making Victor quite literally the "man of her dreams." His youth, vitality, and masculine charisma are unquestionable. In *Cat*, the once-athletic Brick continues to function as an avatar of these qualities despite his alcoholism. Williams's stage directions describe him as *"still slim and firm as a boy,"* and even Mae concedes his magnetism and good looks, if only better to taunt Maggie. Indeed, Brick's refusal to sleep with his wife could only frustrate her so much if he were still sexually desirable; Maggie herself makes this clear:

> I wish you *would* lose your looks. If you did it would make the martyrdom of Saint Maggie a little more bearable. But no such goddam luck. I actually believe you've gotten better looking since you've gone on the bottle.

This also illuminates another aspect of Lorca and Williams's use of the Virile Youth: in both dramas he is unattainable, and as a result he is a source of torment rather than pleasure.

In *Yerma*, Victor's only function is that of the Virile Youth, while Juan serves as the Sexually Withdrawn Husband as well as the Ailing Patriarch. Although we never know for certain exactly how frequent or infrequent their sexual encounters are, there is no doubt that Juan and Yerma's sex life is unsatisfactory. Yerma herself declares, "When he covers me with his body, he is doing his duty, but I feel his waist as cold as a corpse!" There are at least three potential explanations for his remoteness: that Juan's daily labor leaves him too exhausted to enjoy sexual relations with his wife, that Juan simply does not want children, and that Juan's sex drive is characteristic of his family, as the First Old Woman declares to Yerma. It is possible that all three explanations are partially true, and that they combine to bring about Juan's sexual neglect of his wife. And while Brick's sexual withdrawal from Maggie is total, its explanation is no less ambiguous. In his stage directions, Williams himself rejects what he labels "'pat' conclusions, facile definitions which make a play just a play," arguing that "Some mystery should be left in the revelation of character." Thus the question of Brick's suggested homosexuality remains just as unresolved as that of Juan's sexual apathy.

As already noted, the Ailing Patriarch is the second role Juan plays. Yerma indicates this early in the first scene:

> But not you. When we got married, you were different. Now your face is pale—as if the sun never touched it. I wish you'd go down to the river and swim, and go up on the roof when the rain

is pouring down on our house. Twenty-four months we've been married, and you keep growing sadder, thinner—as if you were growing backwards.

While Juan's malady may be nothing more than the result of his relentless labor—although if this is the case, his long hours in the Andalusian sun should be darkening his skin, not the reverse—there can be no doubt that he is no longer the man Yerma married. Despite his weakness, however, Juan has no intention of relinquishing control of his home or his wife, in the true patriarchal manner. Burton writes, "Because she is his personal property, Juan has the socially sanctioned right to chide Yerma for her wanderings, confine her to the house, and summon his sisters to keep watch over her." Juan himself never doubts the power dynamic in his relationship with Yerma: "Though the way you are looking at me, I shouldn't say, 'Forgive me.' I should force you, lock you up, because that is what a husband is for!"

Big Daddy Pollitt's situation parallels Juan's. Big Daddy, too, is a once-vigorous man now wasting away; his physical decline is graphically described by Gooper:

> Big Daddy is dying of cancer, and it's spread all through him and it's attacked all his vital organs including the kidneys and right now he is sinking into uremia, and you all know what uremia is, it's poisoning of the whole system due to the failure of the body to eliminate its poisons.

The parallel continues with Big Daddy's patriarchal status and his refusal to consider any relaxation of his feudal authority, both illustrated by this angry tirade directed toward his wife when he falsely believes himself cancer-free:

> I went through all that laboratory and operation and all just so I would know if you or me was boss here! Well, now it turns out that I am and you ain't. . . . for three years now you been gradu-ally taking over. Bossing. Talking. Sashaying your fat old body around the place I made! I made this place! . . . I did all that myself with no goddam help from you, and now you think you're just about to take over. Well, I am just about to tell you that you are not just about to take over, you are not just about to take over a God damn thing.

Big Daddy, naturally, is drawn on a much grander scale than Juan; the Southern plantation owner is as flamboyant as the poorer Andalusian farmer is reserved. But their kinship is clear, and so is the kinship of their state at the end of the plays: Juan is dead, and Big Daddy faces a long, painful death of his own.

When we examine *Yerma* in this light, it becomes apparent that Williams filtered Lorca's scenario, characters and plot through his own artistic consciousness in creating *Cat on a Hot Tin Roof*. Like Yerma, Maggie must struggle for survival in a hostile socioeconomic environment. Moreover, the three masculine avatars that represent obstacles to Yerma confront Maggie in virtually identical ways. But most important of all, Yerma's ultimate triumph of self-assertion serves as the forerunner of Maggie's, the triumph of an indomitable woman's rejection of compromise and of her determination to empower herself and seize control of her own life, for better or for worse.

SUSAN KOPRINCE

Tennessee Williams's Unseen Characters

Tennessee Williams is noted for his compelling portraits of certain character types—the fading southern belle, the gentleman caller, the wanderer. But one of Williams's most intriguing figures is the "unseen" character— an individual who never makes an appearance in a play, yet whose image is strongly evoked for the audience and whose presence is deeply felt. "Unseen" characters can be found in the works of other dramatists: e.g., the figure of the deceased General Gabler in Ibsen's *Hedda Gabler,* or the mysterious, never-appearing title character in Beckett's *Waiting for Godot.* What distinguishes Williams, however, is his repeated and consistent use of this character type, especially in a number of his best-known plays.

For the purposes of this discussion, let us focus on five unseen characters in Williams's dramas: (1) Mr. Wingfield, the father in *The Glass Menagerie* who deserted his wife and children sixteen years earlier—"a telephone man who fell in love with long distance"; (2) Allan Grey, Blanche DuBois's late husband in *A Streetcar Named Desire*—a gentle, poetic young man who took his own life after his wife discovered his homosexuality; (3) Rosario della Rose, the late husband of Serafina della Rose in *The Rose Tattoo*—an amorous truck driver who was killed while smuggling drugs under a load of bananas; (4) Skipper, Brick Pollitt's football teammate and close friend in *Cat on a Hot Tin Roof,* whose sexual attraction to Brick had

From *The Southern Quarterly* 33, no. 1 (Fall 1994). © 1994 by the University of Southern Mississippi.

to be put "on ice" forever, and who, like Allan Grey, chose suicide as the only solution to his predicament; and (5) Sebastian Venable, the deceased son of Violet Venable in *Suddenly Last Summer*, a homosexual poet who exploited people and who became a victim of cannibalistic murder.

Because three of the characters are homosexual, one could jump to the conclusion that Williams kept them "unseen" largely out of concerns about censorship. After all, Broadway audiences in the 40s and 50s might have been offended by the inclusion of a "visible" homosexual character on the American stage. Indeed, as Robert Emmet Jones has noted, no openly homosexual figure appeared in Williams's plays until *Small Craft Warnings* in 1972. In all likelihood, however, the issue of sexual preference is peripheral; for Williams's primary motive in creating these unseen characters was to demonstrate the power of human relationships, to reveal the incredible hold that one individual can have over another, even from a distance, and even from the grave.

Since his unseen characters never actually appear on stage, Williams is compelled to portray them *indirectly*—to sketch their personalities in a variety of inventive ways. The most obvious way is to have the onstage characters speak openly and at some length about those people who remain unseen. In *A Streetcar Named Desire*, for example, Blanche DuBois tells us that there was "something different" about her young husband, Allan Grey—"a softness and tenderness which wasn't like a man's, although he wasn't the least bit effeminate looking." She explains that Allan was a boy who wrote poetry, a sensitive, vulnerable youth who was unable to cope with his sexual difference and who came to her for some kind of help. Although Stella Kowalski briefly adds to this portrait, calling Allan "extremely good-looking. . . [a] beautiful and talented young man" who turned out to be "a degenerate," it is through the dialogue of a single character—Blanche—that we derive our fundamental image of him.

In other plays, however, the dialogue provides us with multiple—and often differing—views of Williams's unseen characters. Serafina della Rose, in *The Rose Tattoo*, pictures her truck driver husband as "a rose of a man" who was completely faithful to her. "Never touched by the hand of nobody!" she cries. "Nobody but me." But other residents of this immigrant Sicilian community claim that Rosario was "wild like a Gypsy"—that he was a dope smuggler, a gangster and that he had even had a mistress for more than a year. A similar disagreement emerges in *Suddenly Last Summer*, where Violet Venable describes her deceased son, Sebastian, as a gifted poet whom the world had failed to appreciate, a forty-year-old man who was still chaste and totally devoted to his mother. Yet Catharine Holly, Sebastian's kindhearted, but emotionally disturbed cousin, suggests that

Sebastian was a lonely homosexual who used both his mother and herself to procure young boys for his pleasure. Confronted with these radically different memories—these multiple voices—the audience must decide which image of an unseen character is ultimately more credible.

Besides depicting his unseen characters through direct dialogue, Williams artfully develops these absent figures through images of sight and sound. In *The Glass Menagerie* the long-lost father, Mr. Wingfield, is represented by means of a visual image—a blown-up photograph of him which still hangs conspicuously over the mantel in the Wingfields' shabby living room. So important is this photograph that in the first scene the narrator even directs the audience's attention to it, introducing the absentee father as "a fifth character in the play." In *A Streetcar Named Desire* Allan Grey's presence is hauntingly evoked through repeated images of sound: the music of the Varsouviana polka which plays feverishly in Blanche DuBois's mind as she recalls the night of Allan's death, and the single gunshot which ended her husband's life. Similarly, in *Suddenly Last Summer* the late poet Sebastian Venable is introduced through the sights and sounds of his primitive jungle-garden. The garden's "violent" colors, "harsh cries and sibilant hissings" not only foretell Sebastian's barbaric fate, they suggest the poet's spiritual agony—his belief that God is nothing but a savage predator, much like the flesh-eating birds which Sebastian witnessed on his trip to the Encantadas.

Although dramatic dialogue and sensory images help to create a clearer picture of his unseen characters, Williams chooses to go one step further. Adopting his most inventive technique, he repeatedly makes use of surrogate figures—or doubles—in order to portray those characters who do not actually appear onstage. In *The Glass Menagerie* we never meet the missing Mr. Wingfield, but we do meet Jim O'Connor, an attractive gentleman caller who in certain ways is reminiscent of Amanda Wingfield's faithless husband. Genial and appealing, with a boyish smile that recalls the father's own grinning portrait, Jim thoroughly charms the Wingfields—especially Laura and Amanda—and seems to extend to all of its members some kind of hope for the future. But like the absent Mr. Wingfield, Jim ultimately devastates the family by abandoning them when they desperately need him. Unable to form a romantic attachment with Amanda's emotionally fragile daughter, Laura, he abruptly "skip[s] the light fantastic" out of the apartment, just as the elusive Mr. Wingfield had sixteen years earlier. The desertion of a *prospective* husband, Jim O'Connor, is hence anticipated in the play by the desertion of an *unseen* husband, Mr. Wingfield.

In *A Streetcar Named Desire* we are not presented with a photograph of the suicide victim, Allan Grey, but we do observe Blanche DuBois's encounter with a young newsboy who undoubtedly reminds her of her dead husband.

Simply referred to as "Young Man," the newsboy is a quiet "bashful kid" who feels uncomfortable about Blanche's flirtatious advances. "Young man! Young young young man!" she says to him, "Has anyone ever told you that you look like a young Prince out of the Arabian Nights?" Blanche kisses the surprised newsboy on the lips, blows a kiss to him as he departs and then "stands there a little dreamily after he has disappeared." Just like the seventeen-year-old boy she seduced in Laurel—and all of the other strangers with whom she has been intimate—this "Young Man" is obviously a substitute in Blanche's mind for the shy, youthful husband that she tragically lost.

In *The Rose Tattoo* another young man, Alvaro Mangiacavalerro (his name means "eat a horse") serves as a comical, yet effective substitute for Serafina della Rose's dead husband. Like Rosario della Rose, Alvaro is a Sicilian truck driver who hauls bananas. Like Rosario, he is young and virile, appearing to Serafina to have "[m]y husband's body, with the head of a clown." To her daughter she confesses, "In the dark room I couldn't see his clown face. I closed my eyes and dreamed that he was your father!" Attempting to replace Rosario more completely in Serafina's affections, Alvaro even goes so far as to have a rose tattooed on his chest, matching the image that used to adorn her husband's body. "I wanted to be—close to you . . . to make you—happy," explains Alvaro.

A different kind of surrogate appears in *Cat on a Hot Tin Roof*, for in this case a major character, Brick Pollitt, becomes the reincarnation of an unseen character—the suicide victim, Skipper. "Skipper broke in two like a rotten stick," says Brick. "No body ever turned so fast to a lush—or died of it so quick." Yet Brick could easily be speaking here of his own past (and potentially future) experience. Like Skipper, Brick is an over-the-hill athlete, a sexually insecure, guilt-ridden man who can neither understand nor deal with his deep attachment to his football teammate. Like Skipper, Brick discovers that he is unable to engage in a "normal" heterosexual relationship. (Skipper's failed sexual liaison with Margaret Pollitt precedes Brick's own sexual break from his wife.) And like Skipper, Brick has abruptly withdrawn into himself, turning to alcohol to escape from emotional pain, and virtually giving up on life. As Donald Pease argues, Brick has become "the alcoholic and dying version" of his football companion. We never observe Skipper's "crack-up" directly, but we are able to witness it indirectly through Brick's self-destructive behavior. The unseen character Skipper is thus made "visible" to a degree through his close friend and dramatic counterpart.

Perhaps Williams's most conspicuous surrogate for an unseen character can be found in *Suddenly Last Summer*, where George Holly actually makes his appearance "outfitted from head to foot" in clothes that belonged to his cousin, the late Sebastian Venable. As George proudly announces, "I found a little Jew tailor on Britannia Street that makes alterations so good you'd never guess that they weren't cut out for me to begin with!" Tactlessly parading these inherited clothes in front of Sebastian's mother, George impresses us as a heartless man who will stoop to anything in order to satisfy his selfish desires—including hushing up the truth about Sebastian's death and allowing his own sister to languish in a mental institution. By employing George as a double for the unseen Sebastian, Williams thus raises the possibility that Sebastian himself may have been callous and exploitative, especially in his treatment of the emotionally fragile Catharine Holly.

Through these sundry techniques Williams not only manages to paint a clear picture of his unseen characters, but he creates a consistent dramatic type. Indeed, the five unseen characters under discussion prove to be remarkably similar: they are male; they are young (or at least perceived as young); they are sexually aberrant, tending to be either homosexuals or philanderers; and they are frequently victims of violent death. But the most salient feature of such characters is their charm—their ability to inspire an almost religious devotion in other people.

If we turn to *The Glass Menagerie*, we find that Mr. Wingfield is depicted not just as a deserting husband, but as a handsome gentleman caller who enchanted the world when he smiled. As Amanda Wingfield tells Laura, "One thing your father had plenty of—was charm!" So powerful is Mr. Wingfield's charm, in fact, that after sixteen years Amanda still keeps her husband's larger-than-life photograph prominently displayed in her living room. She still wears Mr. Wingfield's old oversized bathrobe; and when Jim O'Connor pays the family a visit, Amanda even puts on the same "girlish frock" that she wore on the day she met her husband. Although she recognizes Mr. Wingfield's vices, Amanda clings tenaciously to her memory of him as a captivating and romantic suitor.

In *A Streetcar Named Desire* Blanche DuBois's devotion to Allan Grey is even more extreme than that of Amanda Wingfield to her faithless husband. Despite the shocking discovery of Allan's homosexuality, Blanche still reveres her charming, poetic spouse, picturing him as the one great romance of her life:

> When I was sixteen, I made the discovery—love. All at once and much, much too completely. It was like you suddenly turned a blinding light on something that had always been half in shadow, that's how it struck the world for me.

So sacred is her memory of Allan that when the crude Stanley Kowalski tries to examine her old love letters from her husband, Blanche snatches them away, crying, "The touch of your hand insults them! . . . Now that you've touched them I'll burn them!" As Stella Kowalski explains, "Blanche didn't just love [Allan Grey] but worshipped the ground he walked on! Adored him and thought him almost too fine to be human!" It is no surprise, then, that Blanche should admire the inscription on Mitch's cigarette case (from her "favorite sonnet by Mrs. Browning"), for the words summarize exactly Blanche's feelings for her late husband: "And if God choose, /I shall but love thee better—after—death!"

Another widow, Serafina della Rose in *The Rose Tattoo*, is so devoted to the memory of her husband, Rosario, that she speaks of their love-making in openly religious terms, not only to her female acquaintances, but to a local priest:

> We had love together every night of the week, we never skipped one, from the night we was married till the night he was killed. . . .
> I give him the glory. To me the big bed was beautiful like a religion.

Serafina even has the audacity to have Rosario's body cremated, in violation of Church law, and to make a shrine out of his "blessed ashes," which she keeps in a marble urn in her home. "Pagan idolatry is what I call it!" says an outraged Father de Leo.

Adoration of a unseen character is also evident in *Cat on a Hot Tin Roof*, where Brick Pollitt describes his friendship with Skipper as "pure n' true," "too rare to be normal," and the "one great good thing" in his life. Brick's wife, Maggie, who is anxious to regain her husband's affections, admits to the notion of a charmed friendship between the two men when she suggests that "it was one of those beautiful, ideal things they tell about in the Greek legends, it couldn't be anything else, you being you." Just as Blanche sought to protect Allan Grey's memory from any profane touch, so does Brick try to defend the purity of his special relationship with Skipper. He lashes out at Maggie and Big Daddy for "naming it dirty" and asks, "Why can't exceptional friendship, real real deep friendship! between two men be respected as something clean and decent?"

Even Sebastian Venable, in *Suddenly Last Summer*, becomes the object of a curiously religious devotion. Violet Venable claims that her son radiated charm and that "he always had a little entourage of the beautiful and the talented and the young!" It becomes clear, however, that the person Sebastian charmed the most was Mrs. Venable herself; for rather than face the truth about her son's homosexuality—and her own Oedipal feelings toward him—Violet clings to the illusion that Sebastian was a chaste, saintly poet. When she shows the psychiatrist Sebastian's gilt-edged *Poem of Summer* (his life's work), she even lifts the volume "as if elevating the Host before the altar," and "her face suddenly has a different look, the look of a visionary, an exalted religieuse."

Williams's unseen characters inspire such idolatrous love not only because they are personally charming, but because they are perceived as perpetually young. Amanda Wingfield tends to think of her absentee husband not as the middle-aged man he really is, but as the smiling young soldier, the dashing gentleman caller who courted her over twenty years ago. Blanche DuBois repeatedly refers to Allan Grey as her "young husband," or the "boy" that she fell in love with when she herself was "a very young girl." Serafina della Rose remembers her husband Rosario as having "a body like a young boy . . . and skin on him smooth and sweet as a yellow rose petal." Brick Pollitt associates his friend Skipper with the virility of the young athlete—the glamour of being a football hero. And Violet Venable even pictures her forty-year-old son, Sebastian, as a man who simply refused to grow old. "We really didn't count birthdays," says Mrs. Venable. "Both of us were young, and stayed young." Anxious to recover their own youthful past, Williams's protagonists repeatedly seek refuge in a world of illusion, clinging to the unseen character as an image of that which is eternally young.

Because the unseen character is not simply loved, but idolized by a number of Williams's onstage characters, his loss proves to be psychologically devastating for them. Indeed, the death or departure of an unseen character (which generally occurs prior to the start of a play) often explains the fragile emotional states of Williams's protagonists. In *A Streetcar Named Desire*, Williams traces many of Blanche DuBois's emotional problems back to the suicide of her young husband. To be sure, Blanche has suffered other misfortunes—the loss of Belle Reve, the deaths of various relatives—but it is Allan Grey's tragedy which has traumatized her most severely. Deeply wounded by Allan's preference for male lovers, Blanche once retaliated by denouncing her emotionally sensitive husband in public. "We danced the Varsouviana," she tells Mitch.

> Suddenly in the middle of the dance the boy I had married broke away from me and ran out of the casino. A few moments later— a shot! . . . He'd stuck the revolver into his mouth, and fired—so that the back of his head had been—blown away! It was because—on the dance-floor—unable to stop myself—I'd suddenly said—"I saw! I know! You disgust me."

Years later Blanche is still tormented by the thought that it was she who drove Allan to commit suicide.

In *Cat on a Hot Tin Roof* Brick Pollitt is similarly racked by guilt over the suicide of his football companion, Skipper. A long conversation with Big Daddy reveals that when Skipper made a drunken phone call to Brick, confessing his love, Brick hung up on his friend, effectively severing their relations. As Big Daddy accusingly tells Brick, "You!—dug the grave of your friend and kicked him in it!—before you'd face truth with him!" Much like Blanche DuBois, Brick realizes that he rejected the person he loved the most in the world, the one who needed him the most, and thus he cannot help viewing himself as something akin to a murderer.

Besides using his unseen characters to explain the fragile emotional states of his protagonists, Williams employs them to set forth the central conflicts of his plays. In *Cat on a Hot Tin Roof*, Skipper's suicide has turned Brick into an alcoholic. "You started drinkin' when your friend Skipper died," says Big Daddy. And the suicide has also touched off a bitter feud between Brick and his childless, sex-starved wife, Maggie. Always jealous of Skipper's attachment to her husband, Maggie is exasperated that she must now battle a rival who is gone, but still hauntingly present. "Skipper is dead!" she cries out to Brick in desperation. "I'm alive! Maggie the Cat is—alive!" In *The Glass Menagerie* another unseen character, Mr. Wingfield, can be held responsible for much of the conflict within the present Wingfield household. Amanda's insecurity about the future, Laura's pathological shyness and Tom's resentment at having to support his mother and sister can all be attributed to the loss of the head of their family sixteen years ago. Williams is clearly interested not in the desertion of the father itself, but in the *effect* of that desertion on the family.

The ability of an unseen character to precipitate a central dramatic conflict is most strikingly revealed in *Suddenly Last Summer*, where Sebastian Venable's death (as well as his life) becomes the principal subject of the play. As in earlier works, the loss of an unseen character has been emotionally traumatic—in this case, both to Violet Venable, who doted on her son, and to Catharine Holly, who witnessed her cousin's barbaric murder. Furthermore, Sebastian creates the primary tension of the drama—the battle between Mrs. Venable and Catharine over the facts surrounding his death. But *Suddenly Last Summer* is unique in that the unseen character Sebastian remains at the center of the play at all times, from Violet Venable's first remarks about her son's garden, to the psychiatrist's probing questions, to Catharine Holly's frenzied memories of her cousin's fate. Indeed, so dominant is his presence that Sebastian Venable, a figure who never appears in person in *Suddenly Last Summer*, actually succeeds in taking over the drama—emerging, one could argue, as its true major character.

Williams also associates Sebastian with the most powerful presence of all, the ultimate "unseen character"—God. According to Mrs. Venable,

Sebastian once sailed to the Encantadas, "looking for God," but what he witnessed was the massacre of baby sea turtles by flocks of carnivorous birds:

> They were diving down on the hatched sea turtles, turning them over to expose their soft undersides, tearing the undersides open and rending and eating their flesh. Sebastian guessed that possibly only a hundredth of one per cent of their number would escape to the sea.

As Mrs. Venable explains, Sebastian was convinced that this hideous spectacle offered him the very image of God which he had been seeking. "When he came back down the rigging, he said, Well, now I've seen Him!—and he meant God." The play suggests, however, that God cannot—must not—be "seen" in this distorted manner, for Sebastian's mistaken image of God has led to the poet's spiritual despair and eventually to his savage destruction. Weighed down by pessimism (as was Williams himself at the time he wrote the drama), Sebastian has essentially become incapable of love—alienating himself not only from divine grace, but also from the redemptive power of human affection.

According to Thomas P. Adler, Tennessee Williams basically conceived of God "as anthropomorphic, made in man's own image and likeness." Williams himself confirmed this view in his *Memoirs*, when he admitted to a friend that he believed in angels more than he did in God: "and the reason was that I had never known God . . . but that I had known several angels in my life. . . . I mean human angels." Perhaps nowhere in Williams's drama is this anthropomorphic vision more apparent than in the portraits of his unseen characters. Whether they are figures of cruelty or of tenderness and love, Williams's unseen characters are invariably presented as gods in human form. Their invisible influence is potent, uncanny and omnipresent. Even minor versions of this character type, such as the homosexual lovers Jack Straw and Peter Ochello in *Cat on a Hot Tin Roof*, are pictured as possessing supernatural powers, having "gently and poetically haunted" the scene of the play.

Worshipped like deities, Williams's unseen characters initially bring happiness and love into the lives of his protagonists—the "love which is glory," as Serafina della Rose calls it. But when that transcendent love is lost, as it inevitably is, the same unseen characters produce pain and confusion, driving Williams's protagonists to irrational behavior and even to the brink of insanity. As the doctor in *The Rose Tattoo* explains to Father de Leo, people "find God in each other. And when they lose each other, they lose God and they're lost." It is this tragic experience of loss—comparable to the loss of one's religious faith—which Williams often movingly portrays.

Despite the diversity of his dramas, Tennessee Williams essentially tells the same story over and over again. He records the yearnings of the loveless, the cries of the desperately lonely. In a number of plays Williams's protagonists long for the affection of someone who is nearby, yet unattainable (as does Alma Winemiller in *Summer and Smoke*, or Chance Wayne in *Sweet Bird of Youth*). But in other dramas Williams's characters yearn for a love that is irrevocably lost, a love that can be called to life again only by means of memory and imagination. Through the device of the unseen character, Williams intensifies the spirit of loneliness and longing which pervades many of his plays; for by making the loved one *unseen*, he suggests that ideal love quickly vanishes, that it belongs solely to a world of illusion. At the same time, however, Williams testifies to the power of the illusion itself—to the preciousness of a love which binds two human beings together and which grants them at least a fleeting image of God.

MARK ROYDEN WINCHELL

Come Back to the Locker Room Ag'in, Brick Honey!

The ideal of male companionship is one of the most enduring myths in American literature. As Leslie Fiedler argues in "Come Back to the Raft Ag'in, Huck Honey!," the works that we most revere tend to be boys' books. These narratives "proffer a chaste male love as the ultimate emotional experience. . . . In Dana, it is the narrator's melancholy love for the *kanaka* Hope; in Cooper, the lifelong affection of Natty Bumppo and Chingachgook; in Melville, Ishmael's love for Queequeg; in Twain, Huck's feeling for Nigger Jim." These books and others like them celebrate "an essential aspect of American sentimental life: the camaraderie of the locker room and ball park, the good fellowship of the poker game and fishing trip, a kind of passionless passion, at once gross and delicate, homoerotic in the boy's sense, possessing an innocence above suspicion." "To doubt for a moment this innocence," Fiedler insists, "would destroy our stubborn belief in a relationship simple, utterly satisfying, yet immune to lust; physical as the handshake is physical, this side of copulation." Tennessee Williams's *Cat on a Hot Tin Roof* is a scandalous, and ultimately subversive, play precisely because it does doubt the "innocence" of such a relationship.

Williams's treatment of homosexuality in *Cat on a Hot Tin Roof* represents an advance over the clichés of *A Streetcar Named Desire*. In *Streetcar*, Blanche's homosexual husband, Allan Grey, conforms to stereotype ("there

From *The Mississippi Quarterly* 48, no. 4 (Fall 1995). © 1995 by Mississippi State University.

was something different about the boy, a nervousness, a softness and tenderness which wasn't like a man's"), even to the point of killing himself by
shoving a phallic revolver into his mouth. In *Cat*, Brick and Skipper inhabit
the macho world of big-time athletics. To all outward appearances, their
friendship conforms to the sentimental myth that Fiedler describes. The
thought that it might be anything more than that is enough to kill Skipper.
It also drives Brick to drink, threatens to destroy his marriage to Maggie,
and endangers his inheritance of the plantation upon Big Daddy's demise.
In the hands of a less gifted, or less conflicted, playwright, this situation
might have lent itself to an angry polemic against homophobia. In
Williams's play, however, homoeroticism is more a personal than a political
or social problem. It is the love that dare not *know* its name.

Because Skipper has died before the play begins, his relationship with
Brick is never dramatized. Instead, Williams gives us at least five different
interpretations of that relationship. These different interpretations serve a
theatrical function somewhat similar to multiple points of view in a novel.
Just as we get a more rounded picture of Thomas Sutpen by seeing him
from a variety of perspectives, we understand more about Brick and Skipper
by seeing the impact of their friendship on an entire cast of characters.
What remains uncertain is the view of Williams himself. In the alternate
third acts that he wrote for the play and the various contradictory comments
he made about his intentions, Williams reflected an ambivalence that finally
makes *Cat* a problematic, if undeniably powerful, work of art.

The most conventional interpretation of Brick's relationship with
Skipper is rendered by Mae and Gooper. They see these two gridiron
heroes as examples of arrested development. In the original version of the
third act, Mae says: "Brick kept living in his past glory at college! Still a
football player at twenty-seven!" In the Broadway version of the play, these
observations are split between Mae and Gooper. In both versions, the
brother and sister-in-law try to convince Big Daddy and Big Mama that
Brick is a sexual deviate. It would be inexact, however, to characterize Mae
and Gooper as homophobic. They undoubtedly support the official taboos
against homosexuality, but there is no evidence that they are viscerally
offended by the thought that Brick is a "pervert." The only emotions that
seem to move them are avarice and envy. If anything, they are probably
delighted by the thought that Brick is the antithesis of the all-American
male everyone has believed him to be. That notion would vindicate the less
gifted and less favored Gooper, while giving him his most plausible claim to
Big Daddy's inheritance.

In his characterization of Mae and Gooper, Williams seems downright
heterophobic. By making the only monogamous heterosexuals in the play

his two most ridiculous and loathsome characters, he invites us to deplore the traditional family. Big Daddy compares Mae's fertility to that of a farm animal, and Maggie refers to her nieces and nephews as "no-neck monsters." A more evenhanded playwright might have generated some small degree of sympathy for the slighted older brother, but Williams is unrelentingly contemptuous in his portrayal of the entire Gooper clan. If this is what the nuclear family looks like, then perhaps the embittered celibacy of Brick or the primal lecheries of Big Daddy represent more authentic responses to life. The male bonding of two football teammates or even the same-sex marriage of Jack Straw and Peter Ochello may be even better.

To see Brick and Skipper only as cases of arrested development, with no sexual overtones, is still to evoke the ideal of male companionship that Fiedler argues is at the heart of our classic literature. The heroes of our boys' books (Huck and Jim, Natty and Chingachgook, Ishmael and Quee-queg) are themselves boys who never grew up. Whatever else they may have been Brick and Skipper were certainly of this company. When Richard Brooks adapted *Cat* for the screen in 1958, he was forced to purge any allusions to homosexuality. The theme of prolonged adolescence was stressed, instead. Brick could not be a husband to Maggie or an heir to Big Daddy because those roles would have forced him to assume adult responsibility. (Skipper fell apart because his athletic inadequacies were graphically exposed when he was forced to play a televised game without the injured Brick at his side.) By enabling Brick finally to assume those responsibilities, Brooks's film manufactures an upbeat ending that violates the spirit of Williams's play. Nevertheless, by making the issue of maturation the crux of his film, Brooks remains in the tradition of the classic American myth and reminds us how much of that myth can survive even the bowdlerizing efforts of the censors.

Brick's own view of his friendship with Skipper is both complex and defensive. If Mae and Gooper are only casually homophobic, Brick is profoundly disturbed by the thought of unconventional sexuality. In Act Two, he tells Big Daddy that "at Ole Miss when it was discovered a pledge to our fraternity, Skipper's and mine, did a, *attempted* to do a, unnatural thing with—We not only dropped him like a hot rock!—We told him to get off the campus, and he did, he got!" At no point in the play does Brick ever entertain the notion that he and Skipper are anything more than good locker-room buddies. He protests (perhaps too much) that, unlike Straw and Ochello, he and Skipper are not "ducking sissies . . . queers." He asks Big Daddy: "Why can't exceptional friendship, *real, real, deep, deep friendship!* between two men be respected as something clean and decent." Then, he goes on to give his version of that friendship:

Skipper and me had a clean true thing between us!—had a clean friendship, practically all our lives, till Maggie got the idea you're talking about. Normal? No!—It was too rare to be normal, any true thing between two people is too rare to be normal. Oh, once in a while he put his hand on my shoulder or I'd put mine on his, oh, maybe even when we were touring the country in pro-football an' shared hotel-rooms we'd reach across the space between the two beds and shake hands to say goodnight.

What Brick has described is "a relationship simple, utterly satisfying, yet immune to lust; physical as the handshake is physical."

Brick is quite right in saying that Maggie destroyed this idyllic relationship by suggesting that it was not entirely innocent. To speak of "innocence" in this context is not to imply that fully realized homosexual lust is "guilty" (although Brick obviously thinks that it is). Innocence simply means a lack of knowledge. A closeness that might seem suspect in grown men is accepted between boys. As long as Brick and Skipper are able to foster the illusion that they are still boys (with a barnstorming football team that is nearly as much of a fantasy as Tom Sawyer's Gang), they are safe in their homoerotic Eden. The fall from innocence occurs with the knowledge that Maggie forces Skipper to consider. She may see herself as a cat on a hot tin roof, but in this particular situation she more closely resembles the snake in the Garden.

Brick blames himself for Skipper's death because he failed to help his friend face the truth when Skipper called him to make a tearful and drunken confession. If Skipper is undone by too much knowledge, Brick suffers from a desperately *willed* innocence. Like the doomed naifs in Hawthorne's fiction, he will not face his fallen condition. Instead, he waits for the alcoholic click that will allow him to evade responsibility. For most of the play (and perhaps even at the end), he is unwilling to accept Maggie's belief that "life has got to be allowed to continue even after the *dream* of life is—all—over." As Arthur Ganz argues, Brick bears a remarkable resemblance to the more obviously delusional Blanche DuBois. Like Blanche, Brick drives a homosexual to self-destruction by withholding love and understanding. (In response, both Blanche and Brick seem intent on righting the balance by destroying themselves.) The audience reaction to their situations would have been different, however, especially in an age when homosexuality was thought to be a curable affliction. "The audience, although it sympathizes with Blanche, can accept her as guilty," Ganz writes. "She is a woman, and had she been able to give her husband love instead of contempt, she might have led him back to a normal life. Brick, however, confronted with Skipper's telephoned confession of a homosexual attachment, is hardly in a position to do the same—short of admitting a similar inclination."

Whether Brick has experienced such an inclination is not entirely clear. In an interview with Arthur B. Waters, which occurred while *Cat* was still playing on Broadway in 1955, Williams asserts: "Brick is definitely not a homosexual. . . . Brick's self-pity and recourse to the bottle are not the result of a guilty conscience in that regard. . . . It is his bitterness at Skipper's tragedy that has caused Brick to turn against his wife and find solace in drink, rather than any personal involvement, although I do suggest that, at least at some time in his life, there have been unrealized abnormal tendencies."

Many playgoers, particularly in 1955, would have thought it strange for such tendencies to manifest themselves in the insistently masculine world of college and professional sports. (In ballet or interior decoration, yes, but not in football!) However, Williams may be doing something here beyond a mere playful shattering of stereotypes. Whether we admit it or not, the all-male world has always had the potential for more than chaste camaraderie. As Fiedler notes, "the buggery of sailors is taken for granted everywhere, yet is usually thought of as an inversion forced on men by their isolation from women; though the opposite case may well be true: the isolation sought more or less consciously as an occasion for male encounters."

Another perspective on this issue was suggested by David Gelman in an article in *Newsweek* when President Clinton was trying to ease the ban on homosexuals in the military. "There is . . . an undercurrent of homoerotic tension in the shared latrines, shower rooms and sleeping quarters of barracks life," Gelman writes. "G.I.s get used to the loss of privacy soon enough, but not, perhaps to the enforced physical intimacy. 'If I'm in the shower,' says Mike Tuttle, a specialist at Ft. Bragg, N.C., 'I'd like to know I'm not being ogled over by some guy.' It's an unaccustomed worry for men. By imagining themselves objects of homosexual lust, they unwittingly place themselves in the feminine role—which may explain the vehemence of their objections." Even if Brick possesses no "abnormal tendencies" himself, the thought that he is the object of male lust raises questions of gender identity that may help to account for the vehemence of *his* objections.

Because Skipper is dead before the play opens, we know of his views only through hearsay. Apparently, the face he showed to the world was as homophobic as Brick's. He was involved in the fag bashing that went on in the fraternity at Ole Miss and responded with panicked denials when Maggie dared to mention the feelings he harbored for Brick. In a moment of drunken candor, she said: "SKIPPER! STOP LOVING MY HUSBAND OR TELL HIM HE'S GOT TO LET YOU ADMIT IT TO HIM!" Skipper slapped her hard on the mouth and ran away. Later that night, he came to her hotel room and tried to prove his masculinity in bed. When that attempt failed, Skipper was convinced that he must be homosexual. It was then that he made his hapless confession to Brick and quickly degenerated into a frenzy of self-loathing. When Maggie recalls her sexual encounter with Skipper, she tells Brick, "We made love to each other to dream it was you, both of us!" Paradoxically, Maggie's body is the one place where Brick and Skipper can experience a blameless physical communion. It has an appeal akin to what Fiedler characterizes as the appeal of the whorehouse—"a kind of homosexuality once removed."

The notion that Skipper's liaison with Maggie may actually be a repressed manifestation of his lust for Brick would seem to be supported by recent studies in gender theory. The feminist critics Gayle Rubin and Eve Kosofsky Sedgwick argue that in a patriarchal society such as ours the primary social bonds are the ones between men. Because these bonds "entail degrees of libidinal investment" that may be mistaken for homoeroticism, men "are chronically under pressure to guarantee their own heterosexual status, to ward off the threatening possibility that their relationships are not, after all, so very different from direct homosexual bonds." (The prolonged athletic camaraderie of Brick and Skipper would certainly fall into this category.) Such guarantees often take the form of "casting male same-sex bonds as relations of rivalry or competition for a female object of desire rather than as directly desirous relations between men." Skipper's misfortune is that for him this guarantee fails to work.

One of the ironies of Williams's play is that its two most overtly heterosexual characters—Maggie and Big Daddy—are also the most tolerant of the latent erotic ties between Brick and Skipper. Brick takes the position that anything other than chaste male friendship would be literally unspeakable, while his wife and father try to show an understanding that he hysterically rejects. In Act One, Maggie describes the affection she has detected between Brick and Skipper:

> It was one of those beautiful, ideal things they tell about in the Greek legends. It couldn't be anything else, you being you, and that's what made it so sad, that's what made it so awful, because it was love that could never be carried through to anything satisfying or even talked about plainly. Brick, I tell you, you got to believe me, Brick, I *do* understand all about it! I—I think it was *noble!* . . . Why I remember when we double-dated at college, Gladys Fitzgerald and I and you and Skipper, it was more like a date between you and Skipper. Gladys and I were just sort of tagging along as if it was necessary to chaperone you!—to make a good public impression—

If the theme of homosexuality is closer to the center of the plot in *Cat on a Hot Tin Roof* than it is in *A Streetcar Named Desire*, the physical fact of such relations is more distant. Not only is there a lack of sexual intimacy between Brick and Skipper, but the very language with which Maggie describes the situation elevates it to a platonic status. The analogy she makes is not even to something as near as the bonding of males in the mythic American wilderness but to "those beautiful, ideal things they tell about in the Greek legends." When Brick accuses her of naming his friendship with Skipper dirty, Maggie responds: "I'm naming it so damn clean that it killed poor Skipper!—you two had something that had to be kept on ice, yes, incorruptible, yes!—and death was the only icebox where you could keep it." The irony here is that literal homosexuality was very much a part of life in ancient Greece. (Myles Raymond Hurd argues that Williams, who had been familiar with classic Greek literature from the age of twelve, based the friendship of Brick and Skipper on the relationship between Achilles and his "masculine whore" Patroclus.) It is clear, however, that Maggie is not being snide or disingenuous in holding up the Greeks as examples of chaste male love. Any *intentional* irony is on the part of the playwright himself.

If Arthur Ganz is correct in comparing Brick to Blanche DuBois, Maggie makes an even more instructive contrast to Blanche. Whereas Blanche expressed disgust at discovering her husband's homosexuality, Maggie offers understanding. Of course, the circumstances of the two situations are crucially different. Blanche stumbles across her husband in the act; Maggie only discerns evidence of unconsummated desire in her husband's best friend. Still, Williams could have turned Maggie into a castrating bitch rather than a seductive cat had he chosen to do so. In "Three Players of a Summer Game," the short story from which *Cat* is derived, the original character of Brick Pollitt is driven to drink and a brief summer affair by his emasculating wife, Margaret. "At the end of the story," Roger Boxill writes, "Williams emphasizes the castration theme by comparing Margaret to an ancient conqueror as she drives about town with her amiably senseless husband like a captive in chains behind her." It would seem that in writing *Cat*, Williams deliberately made the character of Margaret more sympathetic than he had in the earlier story. (For one thing, in the story, Margaret withholds sex from her husband, while Maggie the Cat is intent on getting him into bed.) As he writes in the "Note of Explanation" that accompanies the printed text of his play, "Maggie the Cat had become steadily more charming to me as I worked on her characterization."

Had Williams not found Maggie steadily more charming, he could easily have made her into a female Stanley Kowalski. Brick's assumption that she has driven Skipper to his death (much as Stanley helped drive Blanche insane) seems implausible only because Williams convinces us of Maggie's basic sincerity and decency. Had he wanted to, he could have made her lie about her pregnancy seem as avaricious as any plot hatched by Mae and Gooper. Instead, he presents it as an affirmation of life in the face of death. In separating Brick from his liquor until he satisfies her desire, Maggie commits an act that Williams might have presented as marital rape. Instead, he encourages us to think that she is acting in Brick's best interests as well as her own. (This is particularly true in the Broadway version of the third act.) Peter L. Hays even goes so far as to say that "Maggie . . . gives Brick his life back, and from him, Williams implies, she will conceive more."

The tolerance that Big Daddy extends to Brick is even greater than Maggie's forbearance. It is also more threatening, because the thing that Big Daddy seems to be tolerating is what Brick has tried most aggressively to deny. When Brick protests that people have been suggesting that he and Skipper were "queer," Big Daddy's response is to stress his own worldliness. He talks about having "bummed this country. . . . Slept in hobo jungles and railroad Y's." The implication is that he has seen homosexual behavior and is not particularly shocked by it. (Unlike his son, he has not had the luxury of belonging to a fag-bashing fraternity at Ole Miss.) Even closer to home, he has inherited his plantation (twenty-eight thousand acres of the richest land this side of the Valley Nile) from the homosexual couple Jack Straw and Peter Ochello. They took him in when he was young and poor and made him overseer of the place that he now owns. It would hardly be stretching a point to say that they became his surrogate parents. When Brick contemptuously refers to them as "a pair of old sisters," Big Daddy angrily responds: "*Now just don't go throwin' rocks at—.*" Whatever else one might say about Straw and Ochello, their stewardship of the land has been far more impressive than that of the degenerate heterosexuals who mortgaged Belle Rêve to pay for their epic fornications.

Several times in the discursive stage directions he wrote for the published version of *Cat*, Williams emphasizes the fact that Brick and Maggie are staying in the room that had been shared by Straw and Ochello. At the most literal level, their coupling after the final curtain falls would be a triumph for heterosexual "normalcy." However, the symbolic implications of their act are not so clearly cut. As previously noted, Maggie's body is the one point of sexual contact that Brick and Skipper have shared. By sleeping, with Maggie, Brick may be vicariously establishing a sexual bond with his dead friend. Moreover, the practical consequence of resuming marital relations would be to enhance Brick's chances of inheriting the plantation that originally belonged to two overt homosexuals. Commenting on this symbolism, David Savran writes: "[Brick's] successful impregnation of his wife in the bed of Jack Straw and Peter Ochello would ironically attest less to the sudden timely triumph of a 'natural' heterosexuality than to the perpetuation of a homosexual economy and to the success of Maggie's fetishistic appropriation of Skipper's sexuality. (It is in this sense that Brick's act of making the lie of Maggie's pregnancy true would also make true the 'lie' about Brick and Skipper.)"

Although *Cat on a Hot Tin Roof* challenges the social taboos against homoeroticism, Williams's most vital and most memorable character is a heterosexual hedonist. Big Daddy elevates physical pleasure above all other values. He tells Brick that if he doesn't like Maggie, he should find another woman, even as he himself expresses physical disgust with Big Mama and dreams of a mistress he can "hump from Hell till breakfast." If Brick's homophobia is largely defensive, Big Daddy's tolerance marks him as a man beyond suspicion. (As he reveals in his conversation with Brick, he draws the line only at child prostitution.) Refreshing as his honesty may be in a world of mendacity, Big Daddy nevertheless falls short of being a moral norm. In his treatment of Big Mama, he commits what Blanche DuBois considered the one unforgivable sin—deliberate cruelty. The contrast between Big Daddy's gusto and Brick's lethargy is so great that we are apt to miss the similarities of father and son. Both men have left the marital bed because of a self-indulgent revulsion with their wives. For both men, it is love itself that dare not speak its name.

What distinguishes Jack Straw and Peter Ochello from Brick and Big Daddy is not their sexual orientation but their superior fidelity to each other. The fact that their relationship is never depicted but only described makes it seem all the more ideal. (When Brick protests that his friendship with Skipper was nothing like that of Straw and Ochello, he speaks with greater truth than he realizes.) Even though the "marriage" of these two men might seem to resemble the male bonding that Fiedler describes, it differs from that paradigm in two significant respects. First, and most obviously, Straw and Ochello were not a chaste pair living in a realm of mythic innocence. (Brick's crudely homophobic language leaves no doubt about the nature of their relationship.) Perhaps just as important, Straw and Ochello did not run away from home, or try to escape petticoat government, but lived totally within the confines of civilization. The wilderness buddies Fiedler identifies in our classic literature can find freedom and fulfillment only in the *tabula rasa* of nature. We can imagine Huck and Jim on a raft, not on twenty-eight thousand acres of the richest land this side of the Valley Nile. In Straw and Ochello, Williams subverts the American myth of male companionship, not just by making its homoeroticism explicit but by domesticating it. In contrast, the world of the Dixie Stars seems far closer to the never-never land of perpetual childhood.

Even though audiences have been moved by *Cat on a Hot Tin Roof* in the forty years since its premiere on Broadway, critics and ordinary theatre-goers alike have not always known what to make of the play. If William's treatment of homoeroticism seemed scandalous in 1955, more recent theorists have chided Williams for his reticence and evasiveness. Most observers have been troubled by the playwright's difficulty in achieving a convincing sense of closure at the end of the play. Both the original and the Broadway versions of the third act leave questions unanswered and an uneasy sense that the answers suggested are willed and artificial. We are not certain, for example, whether Brick returns to Maggie's bed for any reason other than a desire to repossess his liquor. If he is just thirsty for a drink, then his alcoholism suddenly becomes the central issue of the play rather than the sign of a more deep-seated malaise. The renewed admiration for Maggie that Brick expresses in the Broadway version of the play seems insufficiently motivated. Williams has asserted elsewhere that Brick "will go back to Maggie for sheer animal comfort." If that is so, he is no better than the satyriac Big Daddy and considerably less honest. Such an interpretation also leaves us wondering why Williams bothered to place such emphasis on Skipper's sad fate and on the seemingly noble legacy of Jack Straw and Peter Ochello.

If the ending of the play (in either version) is willed, what exactly has the playwright willed? He may simply have lost his nerve and returned Brick to the heterosexual fold to placate those in his audience who would have been shocked by any other ending. At the same time, he may be using a symbolic code to tell others in the audience that Brick is vicariously making love to Skipper when he "humps" Maggie in Straw and Ochello's bed. It is also possible that Williams grew to admire Maggie so much that he wanted to reunite her with Brick without finding a convincing way to do so. Perhaps he is saying that true love finally has nothing to do with sexual orientation. We can see it in Big Mama's affection for Big Daddy, in Skipper's attachment to Brick, and in the mutual fidelity of Straw and Ochello. Although it can come in many forms, such love is always a rare and elusive experience. Fiedler concludes his essay by quoting Jim's statement to Huck: "It's too good to be true, Honey. . . . It's too good to be true." Williams ends the original version of his play on a remarkably similar note—with Maggie declaring her undying love for her husband, while Brick responds, "with charming sadness": "Wouldn't it be funny if that was true?"

MARIAN PRICE

Cat on a Hot Tin Roof:
The Uneasy Marriage of Success and Idealism

In the psychological study of literature, it is assumed that a work of imaginative writing is always, to some extent, autobiographical; works of art, like dreams, are seen as enacting the author's psychological states, internal conflicts, and current concerns. Like the people in dreams, the various characters in a story or play can resemble significant others in the author's life, but each of them may also stand for the author's self. The principal characters in *Cat on a Hot Tin Roof*—Brick and Maggie—can be interpreted as representations of Tennessee Williams himself. In their evolution from their first appearance in a short story through the original and Broadway versions of the play, Tennessee Williams has symbolically worked through a turning point in his own life as an artist—namely, the point at which he could choose either to shape his play according to his and others' ideas of a big hit, or to become paralyzed as a writer by the weight of forbidden truths that he lacked courage to bring to light in his art. In this psychobiographical reading, Skipper stands for the suppressed truths, Brick is the artist immobilized by guilt, and Maggie represents the impulse toward artistic survival at any cost. In allegorical shorthand, Maggie is Success and Brick is Idealism.

There is ample precedent for interpreting the dramas of Tennessee Williams as literary autobiography; to support the present argument, we need go no further than his own statements. In interviews in 1973 and 1978,

From *Modern Drama* 38, no. 3 (Fall 1995). © 1995 by the University of Toronto.

he said, "I draw all my characters from myself"; "I draw every character
out of my very multiple split personality. . . . My heroines always express
the climate of my interior world at the time in which those characters were
created." He told a friend who had objected to an apparent portrayal in *The
Roman Spring of Mrs. Stone*, "All those people are me. Not you, not others.
And the worse they are the more they are me." Williams also acknowledged
that some characters are modeled after actual people—Big Daddy after
his father, C. C. Williams, for example, and Maggie after Maria Britneva
St. Just, the Russo-English actress who was his lifelong confidante. This
study touches on such parallels insofar as they are related to the central
concern, which is the way the characters reflect Williams's inner life and
artistic choices.

The study of *Cat on a Hot Tin Roof* as a self-portrait is made more
intriguing by Williams's decision to publish two versions of Act Three: the
original ending (*Cat 1*), in which Big Daddy is beaten down by cancer and
Maggie blackmails Brick into bed by confiscating his liquor, and the
Broadway ending (*Cat 2*), in which Big Daddy accepts his death sentence
with dignity and resumes command, while Brick regains his sexual attraction
to Maggie.

Despite abundant critical comment on the revisions, what they meant
to the author remains problematic. There is little reason to believe that these
alterations were forced on Williams by Kazan, as Williams implies in the
"Note of Explanation" which he inserted between the two versions of Act
Three. Kazan offered to return the play to its original form when he saw that
Williams was not happy with the third act, but according to Kazan's account
Williams replied, "Leave it as it is." Kazan comments that Williams passionately desired commercial success. The allegorical reading of *Cat on a Hot Tin
Roof* developed here supports the idea that Williams actively embraced the
suggested revisions, made them his own, and confidently awaited the play's
triumph. His reasons for later disowning the changes appear to be linked to
the guilt of betrayal, not only of a suppressed artistic vision but also of his
homosexual lovers (particularly Frank Merlo) and of the friends and associates whose support enabled him to continue a productive life as a writer
despite his considerable emotional handicaps.

If we take Maggie and Brick to be warring but married sides of
Williams's psyche, and if we identify the conflict as, broadly put, a dilemma
between Success and Idealism, we can begin to unravel the meaning of the
alterations. Williams has given us not one set of characters, but a number of
different Maggies and Bricks. In July 1950 he began work on a short story
which eventually became "Three Players of a Summer Game." The story
explores the dissolution of a planter named Brick, who drinks because of

some unnamed disgust with his life. In response to his increasing incompetence, his wife Margaret has taken over the running of the plantation, a reversal of roles that is seen as inimical to Brick.

Brick makes a gesture toward reclaiming his self-esteem by befriending a young widow, who, unlike Margaret, is a woman who "wants for a man to keep it"; till now, he says, "I could feel it being cut off me." Brick temporarily retrieves the widow's house from creditors, and they pass the summer playing croquet with her young daughter. However, the relationship is doomed by his continued drinking, and eventually the widow leaves town. In the final image, Brick lolls in the back seat of his Pierce-Arrow touring car, with Margaret firmly in the driver's seat, like an "ancient conqueror" parading a captive prince through the streets in chains.

Although the causes of Brick's disgust and drinking remain unspecified, his alcoholic failures are treated as a symbolic castration. Margaret is implicated in his downfall, taking over his role in an opportunistic, vampirelike manner:

> His wife, Margaret, took hold of Brick's ten-thousand-acre plantation as firmly and surely as if she had always existed for that and no other purpose. . . . It was as though she had her lips fastened to some invisible wound in his body through which drained out of him and flowed into her the assurance and vitality that he had owned before marriage. . . . She abruptly stopped being quiet and dainty. . . . strong cords of muscle stood out in her smooth brown throat. She had a booming laugh that she might have stolen from Brick.

Whatever this Margaret may represent in Williams's life and character, he clearly deplores her dominance over her vulnerable, wounded husband. Her assumption of Brick's abandoned responsibilities is in no way a rescue of Brick.

The vision at the end of "Three Players" of a man who has given up on life continues into *Cat 1*, where an alcohol-soaked Brick haunts the stage as the silent, motionless center of a whole family's storm and stress, coming to life only for a moment to lash out at Maggie and Big Daddy when they denigrate Skipper, Brick's lost love. The unseen Skipper provides a rationale for Brick's anguish, symbolizing for Brick the "one great good thing which is true" and exerting a disabling force equal to the guilt of Brick's denial. The image of impotence from "Three Players"—objectified there as an ankle hurt in tripping over a croquet wicket and, even more explicitly, in the final image of Brick as a helpless captive—is magnified in *Cat* as a broken ankle (injured by a hurdle, or giant wicket) which renders Brick dependent upon crutches. His disengagement from life is evident from the remark Maggie makes when the sounds of croquet are heard from the lawn below:

> you always had that detached quality as if you were playing a game without much concern over whether you won or lost, and now that you've lost the game, not lost but just quit playing, you have that rare sort of charm that usually only happens in very old or hopelessly sick people, the charm of the defeated.

Although Maggie accurately describes Brick's detachment, she may be mistaken in attributing it to defeat. The violence of Brick's two outbursts indicates an immense, albeit suppressed, vitality. His insistence on the purity of his love for Skipper is as powerful as Maggie's determination to secure the estate, and his rage at even a well-meaning attempt to understand that love is as vehement as Big Daddy's rage against mortality. It is clear that Brick's chosen path is resignation, self-abnegation, and passivity unto death. But Maggie and Big Daddy have surely touched a wound—namely, Brick's suppressed knowledge that his homophobia contributed to his friend's demise. All inquiries into his moral paralysis, whether by characters or by critics, lead back to Skipper, or more accurately to his betrayal of Skipper. In the words of Donald Spoto, "Brick's paralyzing guilt is due to his deeper refusal to be true—precisely by open understanding—to a friendship for which he claimed total devotion."

In a stage direction, Williams concedes that *"the inadmissible thing"* between Brick and Skipper and the need to disavow it *"may be at the heart of the 'mendacity' that Brick drinks to kill his disgust with. It may be the root of his collapse."* Despite the disclaimer that follows, we can safely take these words at face value and recognize Williams's denial that the play is "about" one man's problems as an obfuscation, as indeed are his complaints of being forced to rewrite the ending and his insistence on publishing both versions.

Just what is being obfuscated? In this symbolic reading of the play, Williams has attempted to bury something along with Skipper, and it should be no surprise that what is buried there is his own sexual orientation and the debt he owed to Frank Merlo for providing a safe, sane, and loving environment in which to write. Brick's anger can be seen as Williams's anger at a world of theatre and cinema which placed a heavy gag on the subject of homosexuality; Brick's paralyzing guilt may be Williams's guilt, arising from his inability to defy the gag and from his unpaid debt of gratitude to Frank and others whose aid seemed a threat to his autonomy. Williams must have felt that he was no match for the seemingly invincible Goliath of censorship and social mores. Unless he had the resolve to confront the censors head-on by creating strong homosexual protagonists (as opposed to such defunct homosexual figures as Skipper and Blanche DuBois's boy-husband), the only other way for Williams to be true to his lover and his sexuality would be to stop writing plays and confine himself to poetry and fiction, where the boundaries of the permissible were more nebulous. But Williams was a playwright, and not to write plays was death to him. It is precisely this kind of artistic suicide—this extreme form of Idealism—which *Cat* and its revision enable him to avoid.

While the Brick of *Cat* somewhat resembles the Brick of "Three Players," the two wives are quite different on the surface, for Maggie in *Cat* is described as an attractive woman with a long, slender throat and a musical voice. Nevertheless, except in other characters' lines of dialogue, she is identified throughout—in the *dramatis personae*, speech headings, and stage directions—as Margaret, and, like the first Margaret, she takes over when her husband defaults to alcohol, pursuing in this case his father's estate. Flattering stage notes notwithstanding, Maggie of *Cat 1* has many negative traits: her spoken lines are bitterly sarcastic, her cattiness is a match for the venom of sister-in-law Mae, and her acquisitive motives are transparent even to her inebriated husband and her self-preoccupied father-in-law:

BIG DADDY: That woman of yours has a better shape on her than Gooper's but somehow or other they got the same look about them.

BRICK: What sort of look is that, Big Daddy?

BIG DADDY: I don't know how to describe it but it's the same look.

BRICK: Nervous as a couple of cats on a hot tin roof?

BIG DADDY: Crap . . . I wonder what gives them both that look?

BRICK: Well. They're sittin' in the middle of a big piece of land, Big Daddy, twenty-eight thousand acres is a pretty big piece of land and so they're squaring off on it, each determined to knock off a bigger piece of it than the other whenever you let it go.

The discrepancy between Maggie's physical attractiveness and her undisguised greed suggests that in *Cat 1* Williams was already in the process of sweetening an antipathetic character, adjusting his attitude toward her pursuit of the estate and, by analogy, toward his own pursuit of Success regardless of what values or persons might have to be set aside to achieve it.

Although the alterations made for the Broadway production are confined to Act Three, they materially affect the characters of Maggie and Brick. The Maggie of *Cat 2* has many redeeming qualities. The thoroughly manipulative lie that she is pregnant, for example, is elevated to a "desperate truth" when she makes this announcement as a birthday present to Big Daddy. Such changes reverberate through the entire play, rendering *Cat 2* a distinct creation in theme and style despite the illusion that the characters are the same people. Indeed, the earlier, more hard-edged Maggie may be invisible to readers of *Cat 1* who have previously seen a stage or screen production. But it is important not to overlook the fact that in *Cat 2* Williams made Maggie a decidedly sympathetic character, and not only because Elia Kazan asked him to. "Maggie the Cat," he states in the "Note of Explanation," "had become steadily more charming to me as I worked on her characterization." Success, presumably, had become more attractive than faithfulness to a dead and buried Idealism. Williams further states that he "embraced wholeheartedly" Kazan's request that she be made "more clearly sympathetic to an audience."

Maggie's sheer exuberance and vitality make it clear that Williams had already chosen Maggie/Success before being advised to alter the play. As Brick strikes at her repeatedly with his crutch, Maggie proclaims, "*Skipper is dead! I'm alive!* Maggie the cat—. . . *is alive! I am alive, alive! I am . . . alive!*"

By contrast with Brick's stasis throughout *Cat 1*, in *Cat 2* he begins to respond to the coercive attempts of Maggie and Big Daddy to rehabilitate him. In his new lines he admits his need for help and expresses his admiration for Maggie:

> I've lied to nobody, nobody but myself, just lied to myself. The
> time has come to put me in Rainbow Hill.

He joins Maggie in her battle for the inheritance, supporting her lie with his own lie that the two of them are "silent lovers." The thematic incongruity of a lie told by a man who drinks because of his disgust with mendacity supports the allegorical reading, for *Cat 2* plays out the victory of Success over Idealism, of artistic survival over artistic integrity.

The final moment, in which Maggie declares her determination to give Brick back his life, has a tenderness that is entirely lacking in *Cat 1*, which ends on an ironic note. In the original ending, Maggie's lines consist of commands to Brick, assertions of her power, and protestations of love which Brick rejects:

now I'm stronger than you and I can love you more truly! . . . And so tonight we're going to make the lie true, and when that's done, I'll bring the liquor back here and we'll get drunk together. . . . What do you say?

Brick has no reply: "I don't say anything. I guess there's nothing to say." Finally, after she again insists, "I *do* love you, Brick I *do*!" he answers, "Wouldn't it be funny if that was true?"

Like Big Daddy, who earlier made the same response to Big Mama's declaration of love, Brick rejects what he perceives to be a lie, in keeping with the play's theme of disgust with mendacity. More to the point, both men are unable to believe that they are loved, an inability also suffered by the author. In one of many examples provided by Donald Windham, Williams explained the breakup of a significant relationship by saying that "Kip didn't care enough for him," when in fact it was Williams who was unable to believe in or return Kip's gift of love.

The ending of *Cat 2* omits Brick's skeptical line as well as two grim reminders that death is in the Pollitt house—a groaning cry from Big Daddy, followed by Big Mama rushing in to grab the morphine syringe. When Maggie asks, "What do you say, baby?" Brick replies, "I admire you, Maggie"—reversing his former posture of detachment and abandoning his position that Maggie has destroyed his one true relationship. It is this change, far more than the sweetening of Maggie, that signifies Williams's decision to sacrifice Idealism for Success. In the instant that Skipper is abandoned, the playwright snaps the slender thread that tied the play to his homosexual world and the friends and lovers who peopled it. Accompanying this loss is the loss of a broader thematic vision.

Even with its comedic elements—the sitcom nastiness of the repartee between Maggie and Mae, Big Daddy's jokes at the expense of his wife and the preacher, and the antics of the terrible tribe of brats—*Cat 1* presents a serious treatment of mortality, existential dread, and warring impulses toward death and survival; Brick, with his incurable disgust, is an anti-hero, as Esther Merle Jackson has pointed out, and the play a tragicomedy. But *Cat 2* moves away from existential dread to become a problem play with recognizable dilemmas, comfortable solutions, and characters who have a reassuring measure of kindness and nobility; indeed, as Thomas H. Pauly has noted, it bears a much more than coincidental resemblance to Kazan's previous three hits—*Tea and Sympathy, On the Waterfront,* and *East of Eden*—each of them featuring a deeply troubled male whose alienation is relieved by "a generous, understanding woman." *Cat 1*, of course, had turned the formula on its head with its self-interested heroine and incurable hero.

In admiring the unique qualities of both the play and "Three Players of a Summer Game," Donald Spoto describes the story in these words: "Compassionate but calm in its wonder about the mystery of spiritual anguish and emotional impotence, it suggests that there was a latent capacity for almost philosophical reverie that in Tennessee Williams did not flourish." In choosing to alter *Cat* in pursuit of success, Williams in effect turned away from his philosophical bent, but for desperate reasons.

Even before this period, Williams had been afflicted with a keen awareness of mortality, for which his work was the only reliable antidote. A fear of dying "overshadowed his life," according to Windham; as early as age twenty-one, Williams "had suffered a psychosomatic breakdown, his first recorded imaginary coronary." In the spring of 1946, a mysterious and incessant abdominal pain convinced him that he was dying. Even after surgery had removed the abnormality that was causing the pain, Tennessee continued to tell people he was going to die. While working on *A Streetcar Named Desire* in 1947, he believed that it would be his last play; he said the same about *Cat* and a number of other plays. Work itself kept his depressions at bay. In 1947, in the throes of a death fear, he "wrote furiously" on A *Streetcar Named Desire.*

> For despite the fact that I thought I was dying, or may be because of it, I had a great passion for work. I would work from early morning until early afternoon, and then, spent from the rigors of creation, I would go around the corner to a bar called Victor's and revive myself with a marvelous drink called a Brandy Alexander.

In 1953 he suffered from "a writer's block such as he had never before experienced." He was scarcely able to do more than go to the beach or the movies, and his work "lay untouched on the studio desk in Key West." *Cat* was the play he began drafting when he was able to resume work in the spring of 1954. In Big Daddy, Tennessee Williams may have projected his fear of dying and, in Brick, his fear of losing his ability to write.

Those same fears are embodied in the failing or blocked artists in several other plays: the poets Val Xavier in *Orpheus Descending* and Sebastian Venable in *Suddenly Last Summer,* and the actress Alexandra Del Lago in *Sweet Bird of Youth.* Even works which do not include artists, such as *A Streetcar Named Desire, The Roman Spring of Mrs. Stone,* and *The Rose Tattoo,* present people at a point of exhaustion of their resourcefulness, who have all but given up on life.

In each of these plays the artist, or the person whose condition resembles that of the failing artist, has a counterpart character whose function is to keep him or her from totally surrendering to despair. We shall call this character the amanuensis, a writer's helper. These amanuenses do more than take dictation; their functions include those of comforters, counselors, or goads. Like Margaret and Maggie, they will take over if necessary to keep the artist going. Generally the amanuensis has self-interested or even predatory motives for giving aid to the angst-ridden protagonist, as do Maggie and Margaret—motives which set them apart from Kazan's nurturing women characters.

Although the amanuenses as well as the artists in these plays may well be aspects of Williams's character, the existence of possible prototypes in his life is also an interesting point to consider, since he had a number of friends and colleagues who supported him emotionally during his times of crisis. The most obvious example is Frank Merlo, his longtime lover and companion, who kept house for him, smoothed over the offenses arising from his paranoia and narcissism, accompanied him on long summer trips to Europe, and put up with his abuse and infidelity.

Other real-life amanuenses were Elia Kazan and Audrey Wood, the literary agent who "devoted her energies to his career for over twenty years" and to whom *Cat* was dedicated. Spoto says that Williams came to depend on Wood's parentlike aid, confiding his intimate concerns and relying on her to make professional and financial decisions for him.

"Kazan was his talisman for success," in the words of Donald Windham. By changing *Cat* to conform to Kazan's formula, Williams achieved the smash hit he desired. Yet in his memoirs and elsewhere, he expresses more resentment than appreciation for Kazan's influence. His callous treatment of his companion and lover Frank Merlo is well documented, and he distanced himself from Audrey Wood, removed her name from a subsequent edition of *Cat*, and stated in *Esquire* that an artist "feels humiliated by the acceptance of what he thinks is too much domination." The support of others was essential to overcoming his anxieties; at the same time, it was inimical to his autonomy. If Margaret/Maggie may be thought to embody not only Williams's drive for success but also those who helped him achieve it, it is significant that he depicts the character as predatory and self-interested in her earliest incarnation, and as a progressively noble and admirable figure in the play.

One reason for this positive evolution may lie in Williams's relationship with Maria St. Just, the friend whose spirit and "tenacity to life" went into Maggie's character. Judging by their correspondence, they shared as much love and intimacy as two people of differing sexual orientations could enjoy. In an article that Williams sent St. Just "for safekeeping" he asserts that Brick loved Maggie, despite a "sexual nature" that "was not innately 'normal'":

> But can we doubt that he [Brick] was warmed and charmed by
> this delightful girl, with her vivacity, her humor, her very
> admirable pluckiness and tenacity, which are almost the essence
> of life itself? . . . The story must be and remained the story of a
> strong, determined creature (Life! Maggie!) taking hold of and
> gaining supremacy over and converting to her own purposes a
> broken, irresolute man. . . .

These few lines reveal not only the parallel relationships of Brick and
Maggie, Williams and St. Just, but also the equation of Maggie with the will
to survive.

While Maggie's ennoblement could signify gratitude to those who
aided Williams, as well as his own embrace of life and success, his insistence
on perpetuating two different versions of Maggie could be a sign of ambivalence not only toward his amanuenses but toward anything that would
require compromise in return for rescue.

In revising *Cat*, Williams was influenced by market forces, by the
demands of an audience and director, by his desire to live in style, and not
least by his need, in Spoto's words, "to be affirmed by strangers." But on a
more fundamental level he was declaring his intention to stay in the game.

In this symbolic reading, Brick and Maggie represent his opposing
impulses—the urge to abandon his work in disgust with himself and with a
world in which the truth cannot be told, versus the impulse for artistic
survival at the cost of any lie or manipulation. Brick has lost the will to go
on as a football player because he can no longer throw those "long, long!—
high, high!—passes"; as a sports announcer because he can no longer keep
up with the action on the field; and as a loving husband, son, and brother
because he has betrayed one who loved him in defiance of an iron-clad
taboo. His paralysis, born of an insoluble need for atonement, is countered
by Maggie's realism:

> You can be young without money, but you can't be old without
> it. . . . You want money to buy more Echo Spring when this
> supply is exhausted, or will you be satisfied with a ten-cent beer?

In *Cat 1* Maggie pushes, pulls, nags, and finally blackmails Brick into
cooperating in her attempt to produce an heir to Big Daddy's estate. The sex
act that she demands is a life-affirming creative act that readily stands in for
the act of writing, yet Maggie's victory is a hollow one, achieved by manipulation and producing only a temporary gain in the race for the inheritance.
There is little ground for thinking that Maggie will actually succeed in

becoming pregnant after the curtain falls, and her domination turns out not to have any beneficial effect on Brick: whatever talent he once possessed is going to lie fallow or, more likely, wither away like his will to live.

Brick's stubborn resistance in *Cat 1* to all attempts to understand and cure him reflects a certain integrity as well as the depth of his malaise; the self-interested motives of both his wife and his father are all too apparent, and he is not tempted by the promise of financial security. If *Cat 1* makes a symbolic statement about Williams's life as an artist, it is that he had misgivings about pursuing fame and fortune at the cost of being untrue to his vision. In this play he had again broached the risky subject of homosexuality, hinting that the confinement of his art to heterosexual characters was tantamount to hanging up on a lover—a betrayal which could result in artistic paralysis. However, knowledgeable theatre people had warned him that audiences would reject a drama with "no one to root for," as Cheryl Crawford put it when she declined to produce the play. In collaborating with Elia Kazan, Williams had to decide whether to insist on his unwelcome truths about sexuality, marriage, and death, or to sugar-coat them for a larger audience.

Brick's stasis, then, can be understood as grief over the loss of an artistic integrity which Williams, in the very process of revising the play, was setting aside in favor of realistic material and artistic concerns. *Cat on a Hot Tin Roof* plays out the author's choice between suffering paralysis in the face of the unacceptability of his truth and allowing his desire for fame and fortune to become a reason for going on.

In *Cat 1* the artist's capitulation to Success takes place in a posture of passivity and indifference; in *Cat 2* it comes in the form of a gradual awakening to the attractiveness of survival. If the allegory presented here holds true, the artist's resistance to outer control was softening, and he was learning that what he needed was to go on writing—albeit under the restrictions imposed by his time.

Although he insists in the "Note of Explanation" that Brick could not have changed so rapidly, and that such a change "would obscure the meaning of that tragedy in him," Williams did write the new ending with his own hands, solving Brick's insoluble problem and bestowing on Big Daddy a dignified acceptance of his fate. By having Brick express admiration for Maggie, Williams stifled an ethical principle within Brick and within himself: that Brick must suffer for his sin against his friend until the sin is acknowledged and atoned for. In effect, Williams was denying his vision of the void— or simply recovering from it—and trading it for the money and acclaim which *Cat* brought him in abundance and, more important, for the ability to go on writing plays.

Brick's appreciation of Maggie and the uplifting tone of the new ending suggest a corresponding willingness on the author's part, yet his ambivalence is plain, not only in his insistence on publishing both endings but also in the contradictory comments he made afterward. In his memoirs he writes that when people asked him which was his favorite play, "I either say to them 'Always the latest' or I succumb to my instinct for the truth and say 'I suppose it must be the published version of *Cat on a Hot Tin Roof*.'" He then repeats his objections to changing the play for Kazan and declares that on opening night, "I thought it was a failure, a distortion of what I had intended"—a statement that might appear preposterous in view of the play's stunning success, but one which would be fitting for an artist guilty of bad faith with his art. He goes on to describe the creative stasis that followed the opening of *Cat*, during which he became hooked on tranquilizers washed down with martinis when his usual stimulant, strong coffee, failed him. While he stops short of blaming Kazan for these woes, there is an air of victimization in this passage.

Kazan remembers the situation differently: "I gave him every opportunity to override my objections—the Dramatists Guild has rules about such things, after all—but he agreed." Spoto observes that when the play was revived in 1974, "Williams kept Kazan's structural changes (in spite of his insistence to the contrary for years before and after)." If there is any hypocrisy involved in his pose as an artist whose purity was compromised unwillingly, Donald Windham would say that such a pose is typical of Williams's skirting of an uncomfortable self-knowledge, which then surfaces in his works, disguised: "He dramatized his self-knowledge; he projected it."

When read as psychobiography, the plays communicate the most reliable account of those truths about himself which Williams found inadmissible in straightforward discourse. One such truth seems to have been that in 1955 he set aside a philosophic vision in order to satisfy the public's demand for a reassuring view of human existence and to assure his own artistic survival. That he did so with pleasure, he could admit only through the winsomeness of Maggie in *Cat 2*.

ALICE GRIFFIN

Cat on a Hot Tin Roof

Cat on a Hot Tin Roof is a near classical tragedy, in which a larger-than-life "king" of his domain, Big Daddy, with his son Brick relentlessly pursues the truth, despite the mendacity and deception that hide it. Both of them gain stature by the pursuit but lose the fight against death and the race against time. The resolution, as Williams states, is ambiguous, not "pat." But there also is the promise of a new life. Like classical drama, the play focuses not only upon individuals but upon a group.

The crisis the Pollitts face is one common to all families, the death of its head: "I'm trying to catch the true quality of experience in a group of people, that cloudy, flickering, evanescent—fiercely charged!—interplay of live human beings in the thundercloud of a common crisis," says Williams in a comment on Brick in act 2. The crisis cannot be resolved because there is no communication, only misunderstanding and mistrust, between the members of the family. "Nobody sees anybody truly but all through the flaws of their own egos," Williams wrote Elia Kazan early in their working relationship. "Vanity, fear, desire, competition—all such distortions within our own egos—condition our vision of those in relation to us. Add to those distortions in our *own* egos, the corresponding distortions in the egos of *others,* and you see how cloudy the glass must become through which we look at each other."

From *Understanding Tennessee Williams.* © 1995 by the University of South Carolina.

When asked about influences on his plays Williams often mentioned Chekhov. In this, the most Chekhovian of his plays, both individual and group are significant, yet in their relationships they fail to communicate, for each character's vision of another is seen through a cloudy glass, distorted by his or her own ego.

From his 1952 short story "Three Players of a Summer Game" Williams takes the names of Brick and Maggie (Margaret). A former athlete, Brick is an alcoholic, no reason being given other than "there must have been something else that he wanted and lacked." Margaret is an unsympathetic character who resembles Strindberg's women. When Brick succumbs to drink, she withholds sex as part of her strategy to gain emotional and financial dominance over him. Other than a transition from soft to tough, she bears little resemblance to Maggie "the Cat" of the drama, of whom Williams says in his "Note of Explanation": "It so happened that Maggie the Cat had become steadily more charming to me as I worked on her characterization." Other carryovers from his story, which takes place in the course of a summer, are the croquet games and winning and losing as symbolism. The story hints of an affinity between Brick and a young doctor who dies and whose wife becomes Brick's mistress, during which interlude he regains stability, only to lose it again. The atmosphere is that of realism on the edge of fantasy.

In the drama, in her first-act monologue in their bed-sitting-room at Big Daddy's plantation, the more appealing Maggie, desperate to preserve a precarious marriage, compares herself to a cat on a hot tin roof: "My hat is still in the ring, and I am determined to win!—What is the victory of a cat on a hot tin roof?—I wish I knew. . . . Just staying on it, I guess, as long as she can. . . ." (ellipses both Williams's). Knowing that Big Daddy, dying of cancer, has not yet made a will and that Brick is his favorite son, she is intent on gaining the inheritance for herself and Brick. But Brick, devoting himself to drink, refuses to resist the efforts of his grasping brother Gooper and sister-in-law Mae to be named the heirs. Maggie's determination to inherit is as strong as her yearning for Brick to resume their physical relationship, which Brick has broken off. She knows that the struggle has changed her: "I've gone through this—*hideous!*— *transformation*, become—*hard! Frantic! . . .—cruel!!*"

Maggie's background, her relationship with Brick, her concern for Big Daddy, and her antagonism toward Gooper and Mae—all are revealed to Brick, who, in Chekhovian fashion, seems not to hear her, as he is preoccupied with private thought. He has broken his ankle the night before and is on crutches; his only movement is to replenish his drink, as she chatters: "Mae an' Gooper are plannin' to freeze us out of Big Daddy's estate because you drink and I'm childless. But we can defeat that plan. We're *going* to defeat that plan! *Brick, y'know, I've been so God damn disgustingly poor all my life!*" Part of Mae and Gooper's advantage is that they have five children, and, although Maggie knows that having a child with Brick would insure their inheritance, he is uncooperative.

The one-sided conversation mounts to a climax with the mention of Brick's dead friend, Skipper. According to the facts brought out by Maggie in this act, Skipper had a secret, homosexual love for Brick, of which Maggie was aware, but Brick was not. In Brick's absence she had confronted Skipper with this fact, and Skipper had tried, but failed, to prove his manhood by attempting to have sex with Maggie. Although Brick had learned of the incident from both Maggie and Skipper, he blames Maggie for Skipper's death from drink. The act concludes with Maggie telling Brick, "This is my time by the calendar to conceive."

BRICK: . . . how in hell on earth do you imagine—that you're
             going to have a child by a man that can't stand you?

MARGARET: That's a problem that I will have to work out.

Williams observes the classical unities of place, time, and action in this play. In its single setting, the "fair summer sky . . . fades into dusk and night during the course of the play, which occupies precisely the time of its performance," states Williams's "Notes for the Designer." In act 1 Maggie is the center of attention, as she circles, entices, preens, confesses, and pleads. In contrast, virtually the entire cast is onstage in act 2. Because Brick is on crutches, Big Daddy's birthday party (his last, unknown to him) will be held in Brick's room. The injury to Brick, which Williams makes so convincing, is also a theatrical device to confine all of the action to a single setting.

This play marks an advance over Williams's previous works in that three, not one or two, major characters are developed, giving rise to double conflicts, one between Maggie and Brick and the other between Brick and Big Daddy. Williams uses the classical duologue to develop these conflicts in the opening scene between Maggie and Brick and at the end of act 2, between Brick and his father. He employs monologue at the opening, and a "chorus" of children, orchestrated by Mae, their mother and leader.

Big Daddy is the "star" of act 2. As was true with Maggie, his dialogue reveals his history as well as his character. He is big in stature, emotions, possessions. He left school at ten, worked in the fields, became a tramp who hopped off a freight car "half a mile down the road," and became overseer of the land owned by Jack Straw and Peter Ochello, homosexuals who later died. Big Daddy then took over the land and developed it into "twenty-eight thousand acres of the richest land this side of the valley Nile."

The scene between Brick and Big Daddy hit home to so many in the audience who had undergone the same failure to communicate with children on serious matters that they emerged visibly shaken at intermission. (Miller's *Death of a Salesman* had a similar effect.) By the time the two have their talk it is known that Brick's drinking is related to his friend Skipper—more will come out—and to Brick's having failed as an athlete: "Time just outran me, Big Daddy—got there first."

Big Daddy and Brick have talked before: "But this talk is like all the others we've ever had together in our lives! It's nowhere, nowhere!—it's—it's *painful*, Big Daddy. . . ." (Williams's ellipsis). But Big Daddy persists. He wants both to root out the reason for Brick's alcoholism and to confide in a loved one his relief that he is not dying of cancer. (The medical report, which was positive, has been withheld from Big Daddy and his wife, who have been told the opposite.) "Yep. I thought I had it. The earth shook under my foot, the sky come down . . . and I couldn't breathe!—Today!! I drew my first free breath in—how many years?—*God!*—*three*. . . ." (Williams's ellipsis).

He persists in asking why Brick drinks, even to taking away his crutch and withholding his liquor. Brick says it is "disgust" with "mendacity"—"lying and liars." Big Daddy replies that he has put up with lying and liars and pretenses all his life (with dramatic irony, he has accepted the biggest lie of all, that he is free of cancer): "You and being a success as a planter is all I ever had any devotion to in my whole life! . . . *I've* lived with mendacity!—Why can't *you* live with it? Hell, you *got* to live with it." Brick indicates that he doesn't care whether or not he inherits the plantation and tries to leave.

BIG DADDY: "Don't let's—leave it like this, like them other talks
               we've had . . . it's always like something was left not
               spoken. . . .

BRICK: But we've never *talked* to each other.

BIG DADDY: We can *now*. . . . you're passin' the buck to things like
               time and disgust with 'mendacity'. . . and I'm not
               buying any. . . . You started drinkin' when your friend
               Skipper died.

Driven beyond his emotional reserve, Brick decides that all the truth will be told, including the truth about Big Daddy's dying of cancer. He reveals that Maggie put in Skipper's mind "the dirty, false idea that what we were, him and me, was a frustrated case of that ole pair of sisters that lived in this room. . . . He, poor Skipper, went to bed with Maggie to prove it wasn't true, and when it didn't work out, he thought it *was* true! . . . nobody ever turned so fast to a lush—or died of it so quick . . ."

BIG DADDY: Something's left out of that story. . . .

BRICK: Yes!—I left out a long-distance call which I had from Skipper, in which he made a drunken confession to me and on which I hung up!—last time we spoke to each other in our lives. . . . [Williams's ellipsis]

BIG DADDY: . . . This disgust with mendacity is disgust with yourself. *You!*—dug the grave of your friend and kicked him in it!—before you'd face the truth with him!

BRICK: *His* truth, not *mine!*

Then Brick reveals the truth to Big Daddy: "Who *can* face truth? Can *you? . . . . How about these birthday congratulations, these many, many happy returns of the day, when ev'rybody but you knows there won't be any!*" He then retreats—"I said what I said without thinking." Big Daddy rushes from the room.

In the play as originally written and in Howard Davies's 1990 Broadway revival Big Daddy does not appear again. Just before the end, during the final dialogue between Maggie and Brick, from offstage "a long drawn cry of agony and rage fills the house. . . . The cry is repeated." Both the offstage cry and its powerful effect on the audience are reminiscent of classical tragedy.

As if to demonstrate the truth of Brick's charge of mendacity, the third act begins with the family plus the doctor and minister hovering about Big Mama, telling her the painful truth about Big Daddy and urging her to sign legal documents giving Gooper and Mae the inheritance. While they are pressuring Big Mama and insinuating about Brick's drinking and irresponsibility, Maggie attacks: "I've never seen such malice toward a brother. . . . This is a deliberate campaign of vilification for the most disgusting and sordid reason on earth, and I know what it is! It's *avarice, avarice, greed, greed!*"

The play not only adheres to the classical unities, but it also follows the pattern of a well-made play, with exposition in the first act, climax in the second, and resolution in the third. Told the truth in clinical, realistic detail by Gooper, Big Mama replies with acceptance: "Time goes by so fast. Nothin' can outrun it. Death commences too early—almost before you're half-acquainted with life—you meet with the other. . . ." (Williams's ellipsis).

She turns to Brick and embraces him: "Oh, Brick, son of Big Daddy! Big Daddy does so love you! Y'know what would be his fondest dream come true? If before he passed on, if Big Daddy has to pass on, you gave him a child of yours, a grandson as much like his son as his son is like Big Daddy!" Maggie's "announcement" follows: "Brick and I are going to—*have a child!*" Monosyllabic, iambic, the single sentence in ten seconds brings dramatic impact and surprise to the scene and promises a resolution.

In the play's closing moments, with Maggie and Brick left onstage, she tells him that she will achieve her aim of becoming pregnant "by locking his liquor up and making him satisfy my desire before I unlock it!" The "groaning cry" of Big Daddy is heard offstage again, and, in answer to the herald of death, Maggie, who has informed Brick earlier that it is her "time by the calendar to conceive," now tells him, "And so tonight we're going to make the lie true. . . ."As the curtain begins to fall, she asserts, "I *do* love you, Brick, I *do!*" and the play ends, quietly, magically, as Brick's final line echoes Big Daddy's ironic doubt of a simple declaration of love, "Wouldn't it be funny if that was true?"

In the conflicts between Maggie and Brick and Big Daddy and Brick the complex characters of all three are revealed. Maggie and Big Daddy share a fighting spirit, and Big Mama says that Brick "is like Big Daddy." Both Maggie and Big Daddy have had to struggle upward from poor beginnings, which helps to explain their material and emotional possessiveness. Brick's weakness they counter with strength and resourceful determination to hold onto what they love. While Maggie sees herself as a cat, Big Daddy likens himself to a fist: "All of my life I been like a doubled up fist. . . .—Poundin', smashin', drivin'!" (Williams's ellipsis). Both are tolerant: "One thing you can grow on a big place more important than cotton!—is *tolerance!*—I grown it," says Big Daddy. Maggie genuinely cares for Big Daddy and Big Mama, as they for her.

Brick, in contrast to them, has never had to struggle: he has grown up rich, pampered, good-looking, and loved, his parents' favorite. He has never had to face the hard knocks that might have matured him. He and Maggie had enjoyed a happy physical relationship earlier in their marriage; she says he was a "wonderful" lover, and when Big Daddy asks, "How was Maggie in bed?" Brick replies, "Great! the greatest!" His nickname may come from his red hair (Big Mama recalls him as a little boy, "his—red curls shining") but, as the names of Williams's characters often carry symbolic significance, it may also ironically suggest the strength Brick lacks. He is unprepared to face the reality that will face Chance Wayne in *Sweet Bird of Youth*, that, for those who have only good looks and/or athletic ability, youth is fleeting and time, as Brick realizes, cannot be outrun; Brick has learned this the night before the play's action begins, when, drunk, he attempted to jump hurdles on the athletic field and broke his ankle.

The picture of him at curtain rise, then, is of a handsome, damaged athlete on crutches, a drink in his hand. He drinks to escape a truth he cannot face, that he caused his friend Skipper's death. He drinks until he hears a "click" in his head which brings him peace; possibly the sound is that of the phone when he hung up on Skipper's "drunken confession" of love. But, as Brick tells his father, that was "*his* truth, not *mine!*"

Thus, there is nothing in the reports of the past or in Brick's behavior in the play to suggest that he is a homosexual, nor was he so played by the actor here mentioned. As Maggie points out in act 1, handsome sports figures are attractive to both sexes. But some critics resented the ambiguity. In his *New York Herald Tribune* review of 25 March 1955 Walter Kerr charged that "there is . . . a tantalizing reluctance . . . to let the play blurt out its promised secret": "This isn't due to the nerve-wracking, extraordinarily prolonged silence of its central figure. . . . It is due to the fact that when we come to a fiery scene of open confession—between a belligerent father and his defiant son—the truth still dodges around verbal corners, slips somewhere between the veranda shutters, refuses to meet us on firm, clear terms."

In the stage directions for the father-son scene in act 2 of the reading version of the play, Williams replied to charges that the characterization of Brick was not clear-cut enough: "The bird that I hope to catch in the net of this play is not the solution of one man's psychological problem. . . . Some mystery should be left in the revelation of character in a play. . . . This does not absolve the playwright of his duty to observe and probe as clearly and deeply as he legitimately can: but it should steer him away from 'pat' conclusions, facile definitions which make a play just a play, not a snare for the truth of human experience."

In his reply to Kerr, in an article titled "Critic Says 'Evasion,' Writer Says 'Mystery,'" Williams explains:

> You may prefer to be told precisely what to believe about every character in a play. . . .Then I am not your playwright. My characters make my play. I always start with them, they take spirit and body in my mind. Nothing that they say or do is arbitrary or invented. They build the play about them. . . . I live with them for a year and a half or two years and I know them far better than I know myself. . . . But still they must have that quality of life which is shadowy. . . . Brick's overt sexual adjustment was, and must always remain, a heterosexual one. He will go back to Maggie for sheer animal comfort.

Esther Jackson is quite clear in her conviction that Brick is a homosexual and "guilty of a crime, a transgression so dreadful that neither he nor his family dare speak its name": "Williams finds in homosexuality an equivalent for the Greek sin of incest." Arthur Ganz, examining Williams as a moralist, points out that Brick is punished for his rejection of Skipper, just as Blanche was for rejecting her husband, Allan. Signi Falk links Big Daddy's remark "It's always like something [in earlier talks] was left not spoken" to Williams's one-act *Something Unspoken*, in which he "plays with the idea of lesbianism . . . [and] again the handling of the topic is evasive, deliberately so."

On 28 March 1955, four days after the opening, Williams was the guest at the luncheon meeting of the Drama Desk, a New York organization of theater editors and critics. When asked about Brick's characterization he replied, "I think there should always be an element of the unresolved in the theater—an element of the incompletely answered—we should go out of the theater still wondering, as we go out of life. . . . I'm not able to give pat conclusions . . . I don't believe pat conclusions are true." In an interview with *Theatre Arts* magazine Williams said that Brick was not a homosexual, that his self-disgust was the result of living so long with lies.

It is now possible to view Brick's character in the context of the play as a whole and to see that the question of homosexuality is not the issue. The symbolism of games and game playing, of winning and losing, provides a clue to Brick's disillusionment with the world. For a young, handsome athlete the world of games is an ideal one. As Johan Huizinga points out, in "play" there are "certain limits of time and space" as well as "a visible order," and rules are "freely accepted, and outside the sphere of necessity or material utility."

But, as Brick learns, life outside the playing field is neither so orderly nor so simple. His ideal marriage and his ideal friendship are both destroyed when Skipper breaks the rules with his drunken confession, to which Brick reacts not with understanding but with disgust, ending the phone conversation and the friendship. The once glorious athlete is now on crutches. Hamlet-like, Brick now sees only lies, betrayal, sickness, and mendacity in a world that once cheered his heroism.

Arthur Miller views Brick as "a lonely young man sensitized to injustice. Around him is a world . . . of grossness, Philistinism, greed, money-lust, power-lust. . . . In contrast, Brick conceives of his friendship with his dead friend as an idealistic . . . relationship . . . beyond the realm of price, of value, even of materiality. He clings to this image as to a banner of purity to flaunt against the world, and more precisely, against the decree of nature to reproduce himself, to become in turn the father, the master of the earth, the administrator of the tainted and impure world."

Of the minor characters Mae, Gooper, and their five "no-neck" children have few redeeming traits. The couple are at the birthday party to see that Big Mama signs the papers lawyer Gooper has drawn up, so that the estate will become theirs. There is some sympathy for Gooper when he confesses in act 3, "I've resented Big Daddy's partiality to Brick ever since Brick was born, and the way I've been treated like I was just barely good enough to spit on and sometimes not even good enough for that." Together with the doctor, who has lied to Big Daddy and Big Mama about the medical report, and the preacher, "sincere as a bird-call blown on a hunter's whistle," Mae and Gooper personify the mendacity that disgusts Brick.

Of Big Mama Williams says that "she is very sincere." All the characters except Big Mama have egos that impede their understanding of others. She is the only unselfish, loving family member. She is aware that Big Daddy's jokes at her expense are expressions of his disappointment with their marriage. Her own jokes are a cover for her hurt. Her sincerity and goodness contrast with the mendacity of the quartet. When told the truth in act 3 about Big Daddy's condition, she refuses to accept it, insisting, "It's just a bad dream." The wrangling over the estate, Gooper's threat to sue for his share, and his thrusting of legal papers at her evoke an outburst from Big Mama: "I'm talkin' in Big Daddy's language now; I'm his *wife*, not his *widow*, I'm still his *wife*! . . . I say CRAP too, like Big Daddy! . . . *Nobody's goin' to take nothin'!*—till Big Daddy lets go of it."

Each of the principal characters has his or her individual idiom, with rhythms and imagery that flavor the dialogue and deepen the characterization. Big Daddy's speeches are monosyllabic, their allusions are to commonplace objects, and behind all of them lurk the pitiless figures of Time and Death. He is materialistic, in the vain hope that what is substantial can bring the comfort of permanence and relieve the terror that haunts him. He confides to Brick in act 2:

> That Europe is nothin' on earth but a great big auction . . . it's just a big fire-sale . . . an' Big Mama wint wild in it. . . . Bought, bought, bought! . . . It's lucky I'm a rich man, it sure is lucky, well, I'm a rich man, Brick, yep, I'm a mighty rich man. . . . But a man can't buy his life with it, he can't buy back his life with it when his life has been spent, that's one thing not offered in the Europe fire-sale or in the American markets or any markets on earth, a man can't buy his life with it, he can't buy back his life when his life is finished. . . . [Williams's ellipsis]

He also views death in terms that link the familiar and the unknown: "I thought I had it . . . the sky come down like the black lid of a kettle and I couldn't breathe!" Characteristic of Big Daddy is his speech on pretense to Brick in the same scene, a speech that combines rhythm, repetition, imagery, and alliteration, culminating with a five-beat spondee: "Think of all the lies I got to put up with!—Pretenses! Ain't that mendacity? . . . Having for instance to act like I care for Big Mama! . . . . Pretend to love that son of a bitch of a Gooper. . . . Church!—it bores the Bejesus out of me. . . . Clubs!— Elks! Masons! Rotary!—*crap!*" One expects coarse allusions and is not disappointed, but these are in character, especially as he fantasizes about taking a mistress. His earthy humor and love of rhyming ("Was it jumping or humping that you were doing out there? What were you doing out there at three A.M., layin' a woman on that cinder track?") turn serious as he leaves at the end of act 2 after hearing the truth about his condition: "All liars, all lying dying liars!—Lying! Dying! Liars!"

Williams states, "I believe that in *Cat I* reached beyond myself, in the second act, to a kind of crude eloquence of expression in Big Daddy that I have managed to give no other character of my creation." Big Daddy's speeches at times are reminiscent of Hart Crane's simple, strong dialogue in his poetry, like the mother's monologue "Indiana," in *The Bridge.* E. Martin Browne notes that Big Daddy "reminds one of a character in Genesis (perhaps from the less frequently quoted chapters). . . . The best poetry of the play is in his speeches, which distil the wisdom of primitive human nature." Browne, who first directed the plays of T. S. Eliot, comments, "Tennessee Williams's use of repetition to create a prison of words is extraordinarily skilful: words beat like a tattoo on the heart, yet the beat is subtly changed at each hearing."

Just as Maggie's movements in act 1 are catlike—preening, stretching, stalking, purring at times, hissing at others—so some of her remarks to Mae are "catty": "But Mae? Why did y'give dawgs' names to all your kiddies?" When asked by Brick why she is "being catty," Maggie replies, "'Cause I'm consumed with envy an' eaten up with longing." Her sentences, such as this one, are often balanced. There is assonance and alliteration in the cadence as well, in keeping with Williams's description of her voice as having "range and music." A significant line may be rhythmic, anapestic: "*I feel all the time like a cat on a hot tin roof!*" Or "*I am Maggie the Cat!*" she remarks to herself in the mirror in act 1. Her allusions in her monologue are to hand-me-down clothes that she has worn and a debut dress "Mother made me from a pattern in *Vogue.*" Proper names such as the magazine title occur throughout, grounding the poetry in reality. During her virtual aria Maggie is undressing and dressing, putting on sandals, jewelry, and makeup. Appearance is important to Maggie, because, above all, she wants to remain attractive to Brick: "You know, our sex life didn't just peter out . . . it was cut off short . . . and it's going to revive again. . . . That's what I'm keeping myself attractive for."

Brick is the most complex of the three major characters. He speaks little during Maggie's monologue, barely listening, repeating her last words by way of comment. In their talk together in act 2 he is the same with Big Daddy, until about halfway through the act: "Brick's detachment is at last broken through" read the stage directions. His speeches become longer as he outlines his friendship with Skipper, the conflict between him and Maggie, and the final phone call. Contrary to his earlier, detached repetition of others, he now relays the cruel truth to Big Daddy in short words and direct statements: "We're finally going to have that real true talk you wanted. It's too late to stop it, now, we got to carry it through and cover every subject. . . . Who *can* face truth? Can *you?*" He reveals the truth everyone else had been hiding from Big Daddy—that there will be no more birthday parties or "happy returns of the day."

His apology is softer and slower and more convoluted, as if he were trying hard to think clearly, to explain carefully: "I'm sorry, Big Daddy. My head don't work any more . . . I said what I said without thinking. . . . I don't know but—anyway—we've been friends . . . [Williams's ellipsis]—And being friends is telling each other the truth. . . . [Williams's ellipsis] (*There is a pause.*) You told *me!* I told *you!*" The monosyllables of the last two sentences are cutting, like a shamefaced child finding an excuse for hurtful behavior to a parent.

Thematically, the play contrasts Big Daddy's and Brick's insistence on telling the truth with the deception practiced by the doctor, the preacher, Gooper and Mae, and even Maggie. The imagery of game playing enhances both the atmosphere of deception and the theme that time cannot be outraced. In the earlier short story "Three Players of a Summer Game," the game is croquet, which Williams uses in the story both for a boyhood event in the life of the narrator and as an image when he reconstructs the story as an adult, putting together incidents from the past, just as the croquet "paraphernalia" are gathered and packed into a box, "which they just exactly fit and fill." In a larger sense all the characters are players in a deadly serious game, as Williams suggests when he says the focus of the drama is not on the predicament of Brick but, instead, on the group as it faces a crisis.

Sound effects in the play remind us of games: one hears the sounds of croquet being played on the lawn below the windows at the rear. The click of the ball against the mallet may be related to the click Brick hears in his head as a signal of peace and to the click of the phone when he hung up on Skipper. Games and sports recur as images in the play—football, track, childhood games. Maggie's voice, says Williams at the beginning of act 1, "sometimes . . . drops low as a boy's and you have a sudden image of her playing boys' games as a child." The track and hurdles, on which Brick has been injured, Big Daddy sees in act 2 as a sexual game: "I thought maybe you were chasin' poon-tang on that track an' tripped over something in the heat of the chase." Brick replies, "Those high hurdles have gotten too high for me, now."

But time is the real winner in any contest. When he is alone with Big Daddy later in act 2 Brick acknowledges that "time just outran me, Big Daddy—got there first." He says, "Maggie declares that Skipper and I went into pro-football after we left 'Ole Miss' because we were scared to grow up . . . —Wanted to—keep on tossing—those long, long!—high, high!—passes that—couldn't be intercepted except by time" (Williams's ellipsis). Big Mama concludes the game imagery in the last act, recalling Brick playing "wild games" as a child and then reflecting: "Time goes by so fast. Nothin' can outrun it. Death commences too early—almost before you're half-acquainted with life—you meet with the other. . . ." (Williams's ellipsis).

The published text includes two versions of the third act, the act as originally written for production, followed by a "Note of Explanation," and "Act Three as Played in New York Production." Williams's note reveals that director Elia Kazan, with whom the author had worked three times (*Streetcar*, *Camino Real*, and this play) "had definite reservations" about the third act. He felt that Big Daddy was too "vivid and important" to disappear after the second act, that Brick "should undergo some apparent mutation as a result of the virtual vivisection that he undergoes in his interview with his father" in act 2, and that Maggie should be "more clearly sympathetic to an audience."

After agreeing about Maggie, Williams explains: "I didn't want Big Daddy to reappear in act three and I felt that the moral paralysis of Brick was a root thing in his tragedy, . . . because I don't believe that a conversation, however revelatory, ever effects so immediate a change in the heart or even conduct of a person in Brick's state of spiritual disrepair. However, I wanted Kazan to direct the play, and . . . I was fearful that I would lose his interest if I didn't re-examine the script from his point of view." Williams adds, generously, "The reception of the playing-script has more than justified, in my opinion, the adjustments made." Four years later Williams was to remark in an article in *Playbill*, "A director of serious plays must learn to accept the fact that nobody knows a play better than the man who wrote it."

In examining tragic implications of the play, Robert Heilman points out that in the Broadway version, in which Brick seems to be undergoing a conversion, if he also could admit to himself his own guilt for Skipper's death (instead of blaming Maggie), this acknowledgment could make Brick a tragic hero, a "divided man" rather than one lacking "conflicting drives."

With the third act revised to suit Kazan, the play opened on 24 March 1955 and ran for 694 performances, garnering a Pulitzer Prize and a New York Drama Critics' Circle Award. The reviews were generally good, except for those by critics such as Eric Bentley, who rarely said anything favorable about Williams or his plays. Brooks Atkinson of the *New York Times* wrote approvingly: "Seldom has there been a play in which the expression of thought and feeling has been so complete. . . . Although Mr. Williams is writing about hidden motivations and other elusive impulses, he is extraordinarily articulate. Being crystal-clear in his own mind, he speaks directly and vividly to the mind of the theatergoer." On the other hand, Robert Hatch called the play "a charade that spells 'psychoanalysis.' . . . Villainy in the theater is a splendid, stimulating force, but this cold second-rateness seems to me the negation of drama. Where is the suspense, if no soul is worth saving? Sex and death and money preoccupy Williams's characters; in the face of death, the sex is regulated to get the money."

Although the play with its "Broadway" third act was both appreciated and successful, it is clear from the 1990 Broadway revival that the original third act is truer to the characters and to the artistic integrity of the play. It was directed by Howard Davies, who also had directed it with a different cast at the Royal National Theatre of Great Britain.

In the revised Broadway version of act 3, as the truth about Big Daddy's condition is about to be revealed to Big Mama, there is some foreshadowing of the end as Maggie tells Brick, "I'm goin' to take every dam' bottle on this place an' pitch it off th'levee into th' river!" A storm is invented to echo the storm onstage—the kind of theatrical effect Kazan favored. At Big Mama's words to Brick that Big Daddy's "fondest dream come true" would be that Brick would "give him . . . a grandson as much like his son as his son is like Big Daddy," Big Daddy appears. He tells a coarse joke with asides to Brick, who inexplicably has changed into a cheering section. Esther Jackson, who is evidently basing her observation on the revised version, feels that "the gradual change reflected in Brick . . .seems . . . to represent a resolution which is primarily Christian."

Maggie kneels before Big Daddy and makes a speech considerably extended from the original: "Announcement of life beginning! A child is coming, sired by Brick, and out of Maggie the Cat! I have Brick's child in my body, an' that's my birthday present to Big Daddy on this birthday!"

Big Daddy leaves "to look over my kingdom before I give up my kingdom"; Brick defends Maggie to Mae and Gooper; they exit; Maggie spells out to Brick that "I told a lie to Big Daddy, but we can make that lie come true"; and the play ends with the corniest of closing lines, as if written in Hollywood. Maggie repeats the play's title, "Nothing's more determined than a cat on a tin roof—is there? Is there, baby?" Years later Kazan admitted that "Williams . . . knew what he'd written and how he would like it staged. I took liberties with his work to yield to my own taste and my overriding tendencies."

It took thirty-five years to appreciate how much better Williams's original third act served the play in production. The direction by Davies, the ensemble acting of the entire cast, and the setting by William Dudley combined to make the 1990 *Cat* the best major production of a play by Williams up to that time. Several factors were at work. With a long record of experience in directing the classics, experience lacked by Kazan, Davies was able to instruct the actors in preserving the cadence and melody of the poetic lines. He combined sensitivity, respect for the author's intentions, and a sure sense of theater that never departs from or is antithetical to the intrinsic values of the play.

Under Davies's direction the ensemble acting reached heights rarely seen in the American theater, and the entire production set a standard for future productions of Williams's plays. The setting fulfilled Williams's "Notes for the Designer," in which he states that "the room must evoke some ghosts; it is gently and poetically haunted." He calls for "a quality of tender light on weathered wood . . . bringing also to mind the grace and comfort of light, the reassurance it gives, on a late and fair afternoon in summer, the way that no matter what, even dread of death, is gently touched and soothed by it. For the set is the background for a play that deals with human extremities of emotion, and it needs that softness behind it."

Williams directs that "the set should be far less realistic than I have . . . implied. . . . I think the walls below the ceiling should dissolve mysteriously into air; the set should be roofed by the sky; stars and moon suggested by traces of milky pallor, as if they were observed through a telescope lens out of focus." Set designer Dudley followed these instructions almost to the letter (as the original Broadway production did not), adding only weeping willows from the top of the proscenium to the top of the set, where the ceiling "dissolve(s) mysteriously." The moon was a full moon, and the lighting by Mark Henderson contributed to the overall effect sought by Williams of a "fair summer sky that fades into dusk and night."

In the 1958 film version of the play Elizabeth Taylor fails to find the music in Maggie's lines, among her other limitations in interpreting this complex role. She was beautiful and desirable as Maggie, but the vulnerability was missing, and there was never a doubt that she would succeed, against any odds. As Brick, Paul Newman combines sensitivity with manliness and athleticism. The film was directed by Richard Brooks, who also co-authored the screenplay. Williams complained that Brooks "at the end . . . cheats on the material, sweetens it up and makes it all hunky-dory."

The epigraph is from Dylan Thomas and the closing lines of the introduction are from Emily Dickinson. The Thomas lines are his plea to his dying father not to "go gentle" but to "rage against the dying of the light!" In his introductory essay, "Person—to—Person," Williams quotes Dickinson's poem "I died for beauty" to illustrate that "the discretion of social conversation, even among friends, is exceeded only by the discretion of 'the deep six,' that grave wherein nothing is mentioned at all." He says he does not wish "to talk to people only about the surface aspects of their lives. . . . I still find it somehow easier to 'level with' crowds of strangers in the hushed twilight of orchestra and balcony sections of theaters than with individuals across a table from me. . . . I want to go on talking to you as freely and intimately about what we live and die for as if I knew you better than anyone else whom you know."

Arthur Miller comments on the universality of *Cat on a Hot Tin Roof:* "In an atmosphere . . . of poetic conflict, in a world that is eternal and not merely this world—it provided more evidence that Williams's preoccupation extends beyond the surface realities of the relationships, and beyond the psychiatric connotations of homosexuality and impotence. In every conceivable fashion there was established a goal beyond sheer behavior. We were made to see, I believe, an ulterior pantheon of forces and a play of symbols as well as of characters."

GEORGE W. CRANDELL

"Echo Spring": Reflecting the Gaze of Narcissus in Tennessee Williams's Cat on a Hot Tin Roof

In *Cat on a Hot Tin Roof*, no less than in other works such as *Battle of Angels* (*Orpheus Descending*), *The Glass Menagerie*, *A Streetcar Named Desire*, *Sweet Bird of Youth*, *The Night of the Iguana*, and *The Two-Character Play*, Tennessee Williams draws upon mythological analogues to illuminate characters and to underscore thematic parallels. Myles Raymond Hurd points out, for example, that the idealized friendship between Achilles and Patroclus in Homer's *Iliad* conceals a possible homosexual relationship that sheds light on the "equally ambiguous" relationship between Brick and Skipper in *Cat on a Hot Tin Roof*. On the other hand, Robert Hethmon suggests that the idealistic Brick more nearly resembles Hippolytus, someone who, like Brick, enjoys "the company of other young men, and the delights of athletic contests." Surprisingly, however, these and other critics have neglected to consider the similarities between Brick and Narcissus, the mythological figure whose name now denotes a psychological disorder, the kind of illness particularly appealing to Tennessee Williams, whose plays have often been noted for their psychological realism.

The similarities between Brick and Narcissus in *Cat on a Hot Tin Roof* are suggested not only by Brick's favorite alcoholic beverage, Echo Spring, but also by the pattern of Brick's self-destructive behavior. Like the "beautiful" Narcissus, Brick is a handsome young man, beloved by both "boys and

From *Modern Drama* 42, no. 3 (Fall 1999). © 1999 by the University of Toronto.

girls" (i.e., Skipper and Maggie), who spurns the love of others only to "[fall] in love with Echo Spring," seeing there the reflected image of his (former) self. Unable, however, to possess the object of his desire (neither Skipper nor his own idealized image of himself), Brick, like Narcissus, pines away from unrequited love, seeming to prefer death to life without his beloved. Although death ultimately claims the life of Narcissus and threatens to take Brick's life as well, Ovid offers the hopeful possibility that Narcissus has been miraculously transformed into a beautiful flower. Williams likewise suggests the possibility (at least in the "Broadway version" of his play) that Brick has experienced a remarkable recovery, undergoing, like Narcissus, a miraculous metamorphosis.

As this comparison reveals, the celebrated Brick Pollitt bears more than a superficial resemblance to Narcissus, just as his personality traits and behaviors exhibit more than a coincidental likeness to the characteristic features of "narcissistic personality disorder" as described in the literature of psychology. To understand Brick's narcissistic personality and behavior is to understand Brick's alienation not as an existential condition but as an analyzable and treatable disorder. To understand Brick's narcissism is also to see Brick not as a peripheral player in *Cat on a Hot Tin Roof* but as the figurative focus in Williams's "self-centered" drama. Brick is the "self" around whom the action revolves and in relation to whom each of the other characters is defined. Brick's importance in *Cat on a Hot Tin Roof* is underscored by Williams in a stage direction that points to Brick's significance not as an isolated individual, but in relationship to others, all of whom endure a "common crisis":

> *The bird that I hope to catch in the net of this play is not the solution of one man's psychological problem. I'm trying to catch the true quality of experience in a group of people, that cloudy, flickering, evanescent— fiercely charged!—interplay of live human beings in the thundercloud of a common crisis.*

The "common crisis" to which Williams refers is both greater than any "one man's psychological problem" and more encompassing than the limited circle of his most intimate acquaintances. In *Cat on a Hot Tin Roof* the Pollitt family, in which Brick commands the center of attention, is for Williams a microcosm of American culture as it is, or as it will become in the future. In this larger context, Brick's narcissism anticipates, if it does not already reflect, what Christopher Lasch later describes as "the culture of narcissism," a society characterized by self-interested individuals, people largely indifferent to the past, the future, the needs of others, and a culture—in its pursuit of immediate gratification—unwittingly intent upon self-destruction. What Williams describes realistically in terms of a narcissistic personality is at the same time a prophetic image of an American cultural phenomenon emerging in the postwar decades and becoming widely apparent by the mid-1970s. In anticipating this future, Williams resembles "the great artist" characterized by psychoanalyst Heinz Kohut as someone who "is ahead of his time in focusing on the nuclear psychological problems of his era." In the narcissistic personality, Williams discovers what Kohut describes as the subject matter of "the great modern artists": "it is the crumbling, decomposing, fragmenting, enfeebled self . . . that the great artists of the day describe . . . and that they try to heal." Williams's depiction of the narcissistic Brick Pollitt thus provides, in addition to a fascinating case study, a prognosis for the future of American society.

Brick's narcissism in *Cat on a Hot Tin Roof* serves as a metaphor for a complex of symptoms, characteristic of the society as a whole, that threatens the health and psychic well-being of the American people. Recognizing what Lasch describes as a fundamental shift in the cultural climate from the religious to the therapeutic, Williams, in his dramatic work, frequently depicts a group of people in conflict, the result of a psychological crisis experienced by one of the group members. Laura Wingfield in *The Glass Menagerie*, Blanche DuBois in *A Streetcar Named Desire*, Alma Winemiller in *Summer and Smoke*, and, of course, Brick Pollitt in *Cat on a Hot Tin Roof* are all illustrative examples. Williams also typically envisions the solution to the crisis in terms of recovery or cure. In *Cat on a Hot Tin Roof*, Brick's alcoholism is a symptom that masks his underlying personality disorder but nevertheless signals to Maggie and others that Brick is in need of treatment. Optimistically hoping that Brick will recover himself, and thus avoid the social stigma attached to institutionalization for alcoholism or mental illness, Maggie threatens Brick with the prospect of confinement at Rainbow Hill, a "[p]lace [. . .] famous for treatin' alcoholics an['] dope fiends." Brick, on the other hand, prefers to believe that alcohol provides the only therapy he needs. When the percentage of alcohol in his bloodstream reaches precisely the right level, he experiences what he describes as a "click in [his] head" that results in a "peaceful" feeling. Anxiety-ridden and longing for peace, Brick is a dramatic prefiguration of Lasch's "psychological man," one of the defining figures of twentieth-century American culture: "Plagued by anxiety, depression, vague discontents, a sense of inner emptiness, the 'psychological man' of the twentieth century seeks neither individual self-aggrandizement nor spiritual transcendence but peace of mind." For Lasch, psychological man is virtually synonymous with the "new narcissist," someone who is constantly searching for meaning in life, always seeking the approbation of others, and, like the mythical Narcissus, perpetually living "in a state of restless, perpetually unsatisfied desire."

Attempts to define the psychological nature of the narcissistic personality began as early as the late nineteenth century, when "Havelock Ellis first attached a psychological sense to the word narcissism in 1898 in reference to autoeroticism." Since then, Sigmund Freud, Heinz Kohut, Otto F. Kernberg, Christopher Lasch, and many others have contributed significantly to the ongoing discussion of narcissism. Despite conflicting opinions among the leading thinkers, the American Psychiatric Association in 1987 reached consensus on nine general "diagnostic criteria" for the identification of narcissistic personality disorder, any five of which are sufficient to indicate the disorder. From among this group, at least six of the criteria are relevant to the relationships dramatized in *Cat on a Hot Tin Roof* as well as to the relationship between the artist, Tennessee Williams, and his audience. They include (1) "a grandiose sense of self-importance"; (2) a preoccupation "with fantasies of unlimited success, power, brilliance, beauty, or *ideal love*" (emphasis added); (3) a desire for "constant attention and admiration"; (4) "feelings of rage, shame, or humiliation" in response to criticism; and (5) a "lack of empathy: [the] inability to recognize and experience how others feel." Invoking the image of Narcissus and casting Brick Pollitt in the role of his mythological counterpart, Tennessee Williams obviously invites a comparison between Brick and Narcissus. At a more implicit level, Williams suggests that the specific symptoms of Brick's narcissism, which we recognize in the diagnostic criteria codified by the American Psychiatric Association, motivate the psychological crisis that significantly alters Brick's relationships with his wife, his father, and his closest friend, a crisis that ultimately determines the outcome of the conflict dramatized in *Cat on a Hot Tin Roof.*

Brick's "sense of self-importance" and unique status in the Pollitt family, a first symptom of his narcissistic personality, is confirmed by reports from the other characters. He is, for example, according to his sister-in-law, Mae, a "beautiful athlete," having achieved fame first as a professional football star and then as a sports announcer. Attesting also to Brick's physical attractiveness, Maggie describes him as a "superior creature!" and a "godlike being!" In his study of pathological narcissism, Otto F. Kernberg notes that the family histories of narcissistic patients often "reveal that each patient possessed some inherent quality which could have objectively aroused the envy or admiration of others." As the baby boy in the family, Brick has, since his birth, been the favorite of both Big Mama and Big Daddy and a source of resentment to his older brother, Gooper. As Gooper confesses, "I've resented Big Daddy's partiality to Brick ever since Brick was born." Whenever Gooper and Mae are in the company of Brick, their tone of voice reflects their animosity and jealousy. In the third act, when Brick "*enters from the gallery,*" they announce his entrance with mocking irony, first Mae: "Behold the conquering hero comes!" and then Gooper: "The fabulous Brick Pollitt!" As Kernberg adds, narcissistic children "often occupy a pivotal point in their family structure, such as being the only child, . . . or the one who is supposed to fulfill the family aspirations." While Brick is not the only child in the Pollitt family, Big Mama nevertheless refers to Brick as her "*only son.*" Likewise, Big Daddy shows a preference for Brick by suggesting that he, and he alone, stands to inherit his sizable estate. Brick's own sense of self-importance is illustrated by an ironic deference towards members of his family while he remains the focus of attention. When, for example, Brick arrives on the scene in Act Three, he mockingly defers to Maggie, allowing her to enter the room before him; he then serves himself a drink—before all of the others—consciously aware that he has always been first in importance:

> *Brick smiles and bows slightly, making a burlesque gesture of gallantry for Maggie to pass before him into the room. Then he hobbles on his crutch directly to the liquor cabinet and there is absolute silence, with everybody looking at Brick as everybody has always looked at Brick when he spoke or moved or appeared. One by one he drops ice cubes in his glass, then suddenly, but not quickly, looks back over his shoulder with a wry, charming smile, and says:* "I'm sorry! Anyone else?"

Although Brick contributes little to the family dialogue, he nevertheless commands the attention of his family members and exercises control over their hopes for the future. Principally by refusing to cooperate, Brick manipulates both Maggie and Big Daddy and is able to frustrate their plans. By refusing to sleep with his wife, for example, Brick makes it impossible for Maggie to bear his child. At the same time, by rejecting Maggie's appeals, he also frustrates his father's desire to leave his estate to Brick. Unless Brick chooses to cooperate by reforming his behavior and producing an heir, Big Daddy cannot, with good conscience, bequeath to Brick and Maggie his property and his legacy. In relation to the narcissistic personality, all other family members assume a role secondary in importance. At the same time, they mirror one aspect of Brick's narcissistic personality by insisting that Brick take notice of them and give heed to the special nature of their problems.

Brick's fantasy of ideal love, a second characteristic symptom linking him with narcissistic personality disorder, is something that he holds on to even as others, on a more realistic plane, go about the business of living. Describing Brick's relationship with Skipper, Maggie remarks that "[i]t was one of those beautiful, ideal things they tell about in the Greek legends," but she also reminds Brick that "life has got to be allowed to continue even after the *dream* of life is—all—over." Following the death of his beloved friend, Brick clings tenaciously to the memory of what he and Skipper once shared: "One man has one great good thing in his life. One great good true thing which is true!—I had friendship with Skipper." Even if Brick's ideal of friendship conceals an unacknowledged homosexual desire, it is unlikely, considering the moral climate of the day as well as Brick's narcissistic personality, that he would admit to anything other than what is socially acceptable. As Kernberg remarks, "[n]arcissistic patients characteristically adapt themselves to the moral demands of their environment because they are afraid of the attacks to which they would be subjected if they do not conform, and because this submission seems to be the price they have to pay for glory and admiration." To illustrate, Brick's conventional morality is reflected in his shocked response to his father's more tolerant attitude toward homosexuality: "Don't you know how people *feel* about things like that? How, how *disgusted* they are by things like that?"

Brick's ideal of friendship, as this homophobic tirade indicates, incorporates a view of homosexuality that condemns it as morally wrong; thus, to characterize Brick merely as an example of frustrated homosexual desire or merely as an idealist may be to over-simplify the complexity of his character. Although critics have generally considered Brick's idealism and his (alleged) homosexuality as adequate to explain his character, each of these traits is subsumed by the broader classification of his personality as narcissistic. As it turns out, Brick's narcissistic personality disorder affects not only relationships within the family but also his interactions with people outside that circle, including the narcissist's choice of love-objects. In *Cat on a Hot Tin Roof,* Williams shrouds the relationship between Brick and Skipper in mystery, writing in a stage direction that *"[s]ome mystery should be left in the revelation of character in a play, just as a great deal of mystery is always left in the revelation of character in life."* Critics attempting to define this relationship more unambiguously have suggested, on the one hand, that Brick is faithful to an ideal of friendship or, on the other hand, that he refuses to acknowledge his own homosexual desire for Skipper. In fact, these two aspects of Brick's personality may be conjoined by considering Brick's narcissistic disorder.

Since Freud's earliest writing on the subject, homosexuality and narcissism have been inextricably linked. Characterizing homosexuals, Freud writes that "[t]hey are plainly seeking *themselves* as a love-object, and are exhibiting a type of object-choice which must be termed 'narcissistic.'" Although Freud would subsequently modify his thinking about the relationship between homosexuality and narcissism, later psychiatrists have followed his lead in trying to define their relationship. Kernberg, for example, writes that in "the most severe type of" homosexuality, "the homosexual partner is 'loved' as an extension of the patient's own pathological grandiose self, and hence we find the relation, not from self to object, nor from object to self, but from (pathological grandiose) self to self." Of course, only in the last decades of the twentieth century have physicians and psychiatrists challenged the view that homosexuality is a kind of illness. According to Vern and Bonnie Bullough, it was not until 1974, for example, that "the American Psychiatric Association removed homosexuality from the category of pathological illness." However, in the context of prevailing views of homosexuality at the time *Cat on a Hot Tin Roof* was first performed in 1955, what Williams depicts as a possible homosexual relationship between Brick and Skipper can be interpreted as a pathological manifestation of Brick's narcissistic self-love. To the extent that Skipper reflects what Brick "himself is . . . what he himself was, . . . [or] what he himself would like to be," he is someone that Brick may love, just as the narcissist also loves himself.

Brick's desire for "constant attention and admiration," a third symptom of his narcissistic personality disorder, suggests not only that Brick depends upon others to supply his want of self-esteem but also that he desires, despite some outward appearances to the contrary, contact with others. His "one-man track meet," "stag[ed]" on the high school athletic field the night before the action of the play begins, succeeds in attracting attention to Brick, especially after he falls and breaks his ankle while attempting to jump the high hurdles. By the next morning, Brick is the subject of a "human interest story" that appears in the *Clarksdale Register.* Within the Pollitt family, he is either the object of sympathy because of his "crippled" condition or the object of ridicule because of his senseless behavior. In any case, he is once again the object of attention.

"Because the narcissist has so few inner resources," Lasch explains, "he looks to others to validate his sense of self. He needs to be admired for his beauty, charm, celebrity, or power—attributes that usually fade with time," Brick's return to the athletic stadium, itself a symbol of his former glory, is an attempt to relive in fantasy the celebrity he once enjoyed as an athlete. In contrast with Brick's career as a professional football star, his job as a sportscaster fails to provide him with the "[s]elf-confirming attention from others" that is "one of [the narcissist's] most compelling needs." Instead of finding satisfaction in the broadcasting booth, Brick (the observer rather than the observed) envies the performers on the field, who remind him of his former, younger self. In a conversation with Big Daddy, Brick reveals not only his disenchantment with sportscasting and his reason for quitting, but also his realization that time has defeated him, has removed him from the spotlight of attention:

> Sit in a box watching a game I can't play? Describing what I can't do while players do it? Sweating out their disgust and confusion in contests I'm not fit for? Drinkin' a coke, half bourbon, so I can stand it? That's no goddam good any more, no help—time just outran me, Big Daddy—got there first . . .

In the fading light of his brilliant athletic career, and dissatisfied with both wife and job, Brick resembles the aging narcissist described by Lasch: "Unable to achieve satisfying sublimations in the form of love and work, he finds that he has little to sustain him when youth passes him by."

In addition to exhibitions of the dramatic kind, Brick stages more subtle appeals for sympathy and attention by consuming alcohol at an alarming rate. For Brick, drinking is one kind of social activity that allows him to remain in close physical proximity with others (for the benefit of their attention) while keeping himself emotionally distant. As when he showers and leaves the bathroom door "*half open*," his drinking expresses the narcissist's "deep-rooted needs for empathic responsiveness and for a sense of connection with others."

Brick's indifference to others and his enraged response to perceived criticism resembles a fourth symptom that also describes the narcissistic personality disorder. Williams notes in one stage direction that "*[a] tone of politely feigned interest, masking indifference, or worse, is characteristic of [Brick's] speech with Margaret.*" In other stage directions, Williams uses synonymous words or phrases to describe Brick's indifference. Sometimes he is "*unengaged*," other times he is "*aloof*," but almost always, "*[h]e has the additional charm of that cool air of detachment that people have who have given up the struggle.*"

Brick's indifference is further dramatized by his refusal or inability to listen. Maggie repeatedly asks Brick if he is listening to her, finally (near the end of the first act) delivering this exasperated outcry: "Are you listening to me? Are you? Are you LISTENING TO ME!" His mother also has to ask, "Can you hear me, son?" while Big Daddy, too, has to implore Brick to "listen to [him]." Underlying Brick's hearing problem is a lack of empathy for others. Like the narcissistic personality, Brick simply doesn't care about anyone else's feelings but his own. "[I]t's hard for me," he says, "to understand how anybody could care if he lived or died or was dying or cared about anything." Focusing exclusively on his own problem, Brick's narcissistic gaze prevents him from seeing a point of view other than his own. As a result, he acts indifferently toward others, with the result that he damages his interpersonal relationships.

Brick's rage, like his indifference to others, is another manifestation of his narcissistic personality. In the course of the play, Brick frequently responds with rage to Maggie and Big Daddy, and in each instance, the motivation for the feeling can be traced backward in time to his failed relationship with Skipper. Early in the first act of the play, for example, when Brick accidentally drops his crutch and Maggie offers to help him, saying, "Lean on my shoulder," Brick replies: "*I don't want to lean on your shoulder, I want my crutch!*" In a stage direction immediately following, Williams writes that "*[t]his is spoken like sudden lightning.*" To most observers, Brick's response is extreme, especially considering the circumstances, but his behavior is fairly typical of the narcissistic personality. As Heinz Kohut observes, what is "remarkable" about the narcissist's response is "the intensity of the upset" in contrast with "the content of the precipitating occurrence." Prior to Brick's outburst, Maggie had broached the topic of Brick's relationship with Skipper, chiding Brick for his silence:

> When something is festering in your memory or your imagination, laws of silence don't work, it's just like shutting a door and locking it on a house on fire in hope of forgetting that the house is burning. But not facing a fire doesn't put it out. Silence about a thing just magnifies it. It grows and festers in silence, becomes malignant. . . .

As Maggie's diagnosis suggests, Brick's problem and the rage that it motivates originate when his relationship with Skipper changes. When Skipper fails to conform to Brick's fantasy of ideal friendship by confessing his homosexual desire to Brick on the telephone, Brick's own secure heterosexual self-image is challenged. Consequently, Brick suffers a narcissistic injury of the type "that threaten[s] the cohesion of the self." According to Kohut, it is "an injury to the self" that is primarily responsible for motivating narcissistic or destructive rage.

Following Skipper's telephone confession, to which Brick responds by hanging up on him, Brick not only suffers the loss of a love-object but also experiences shame and, as Big Daddy later points out, "disgust with [him]self." As the American Psychiatric Association notes, "feelings of rage, shame, or humiliation" are evidence of narcissistic personality disorder. With each reminder of the emotionally painful episode with Skipper, Brick experiences a renewed sense of shame. The narcissistic personality typically "respond[s] to a potentially shame-provoking situation" in one of two ways:

"either with shamefaced withdrawal (flight) or with narcissistic rage (fight)." With both Maggie and Big Daddy, Brick's typical response is rage.

When Maggie, for example, brings up the subject of Skipper a third time in Act One, Brick angrily threatens her with his crutch: "Maggie, you want me to hit you with this crutch? Don't you know I could kill you with this crutch?" Moments later, as Williams notes in a stage direction, *"Brick strikes at her with [the] crutch, a blow that shatters the gemlike lamp on the table."* Brick's violent expression of rage is motivated first by a sense of injury to his self and secondly by a desire for revenge. Kohut remarks that "[t]he need for revenge, for righting a wrong, for undoing a hurt" is a characteristic feature of narcissistic rage. When Big Daddy also brings up the subject of Skipper suggesting to Brick that his "disgust with mendacity is disgust with [him]self," Brick likewise exacts his revenge upon Big Daddy. *"[W]ithout knowing that he has made [the] decision,"* Brick proceeds to tell his father that he is dying of cancer, a choice motivated by revenge: *"Only this could even the score between them: one inadmissible thing in return for another."*

According to the American Psychiatric Association, the narcissistic personality also "takes advantage of others" and suffers from a "lack of empathy." Exhibiting both of these characteristics (a fifth and sixth symptom from the APA's list of nine), Brick takes advantage of Maggie's feelings by refusing to sleep with her and shows a lack of empathy for Big Daddy by revealing the truth about his fatal condition. In an earlier edition of the *Diagnostic and Statistical Manual of Mental Disorders*, these criteria were grouped with two other "disturbances in interpersonal relationships": (1) expecting "special favors without assuming reciprocal responsibilities" and (2) experiencing "relationships that characteristically alternate between the extremes of over-idealization and devaluation." Only the last of these items is not a separate criterion in the revised 1987 list of diagnostic criteria, but it, too, usefully parallels the way Brick values and then devalues his relationship with Skipper. Brick's lack of empathy, his manipulation of others, and his widely fluctuating emotional responses all indicate a severe disturbance of normal interpersonal relationships.

To this list of five symptoms Lasch would add that the typical narcissist has little concern for what happens in the future. Instead, the narcissist focuses on the present moment, indulging in gratifying his or her immediate desires. Brick's lack of interest in the future is reflected by his reluctance to father a child. As Lasch explains, the narcissist "takes no interest in the future and does nothing to provide himself with the traditional consolations of old age, the most important of which is the belief that future generations will in some sense carry on his life's work." Instead, Brick looks backward to a more glorious time in his own self-history, to a period when he was young and the center of attention. As Lasch explains, narcissists "wish for eternal youth, for the same reason they no longer care to reproduce themselves."

Apart from contributing to a realistic depiction of the narcissistic personality, the symptoms that characterize Brick Pollitt in *Cat on a Hot Tin Roof* serve an important signifying function. As Jacques Lacan explains, the symptom is "a metaphor in which flesh or function is taken as a signifying element." For the analyst, to diagnose the symptom is to gain access to what is "inaccessible to the conscious subject," often a "sexual trauma" in the patient's history of desire. In the case of Brick, self-reflection does not lead to self-revelation. Limited by his narcissistic gaze, Brick is unable to see that his current state of melancholy stems not from the death of Skipper but from his rejection of Skipper's friendship and love. Brick's narcissistic symptoms thus take on their pathological aspect prior to Skipper's death and immediately following the telephone conversation in which Skipper confesses his love to Brick. After that traumatic moment, Brick's desire, which had always been for a purely idealistic relationship, comes to an abrupt end with the knowledge that Skipper (and only Skipper, according to Maggie) "harbored even any *unconscious* desire for anything not perfectly pure" in the way of a relationship between the two men. Brick suffers not from grief, which dissipates with time, but from a more serious disorder of the self, one that threatens to resolve itself only in his death.

In the original version of *Cat on a Hot Tin Roof*, before Tennessee Williams revised the third act and incorporated director Elia Kazan's suggested changes, Brick's projected fate is similar to that of Narcissus. In Ovid's story, although death comes to Narcissus, it provides no relief from his suffering: "[E]ven in Hell," Ovid writes, "he found a pool to gaze in,/ Watching his image in the Stygian water." Similarly, the original *Cat on a Hot Tin Roof* concludes with no suggestion that Brick's condition has changed or will ever change. In the concluding scene, although Maggie vows, "we're going to make the lie true," meaning that she and Brick "are going to—*have a child!*" Brick remains opposed to the idea, asking Maggie: "how are you going to conceive a child by a man in love with his liquor?" Persistent as always, Maggie makes a final appeal: "I *do* love you, Brick I *do!*" but Brick's reply, "Wouldn't it be funny if that was true?" again suggests a pessimistic outcome.

In the revised "Broadway version" of *Cat on a Hot Tin Roof*, Williams offers an alternative reading of the Ovidian myth in which he exploits the optimistic possibilities suggested by the notion of metamorphosis and by the apparent transformation of Narcissus into a flower. In the eyes of critics who see the change in Brick's character coming about too rapidly, the transformation seems to be, like that of Narcissus, simply miraculous. Among the significant changes in the "Broadway version," the suddenly self-aware Brick Pollitt admits, for example, that he has "lied to [him]self" about his alcoholic condition. In contrast to the original version, in the "Broadway version" Brick is willing to commit himself to Rainbow Hill for treatment. No longer indifferent in the "Broadway version"'s third act, Brick defends Maggie against the accusations of Mae and Gooper, even though he knows Maggie is lying: "No, truth is something desperate, an' she's got it." In the concluding scene, Brick confesses, "I admire you, Maggie," suggesting a much more hopeful outcome than in the original third act. As if to confirm that Brick has recovered from his narcissistic personality disorder, Maggie reports, after destroying Brick's liquor supply, that "Echo Spring has gone dry."

Whether from the perspective of the American Psychiatric Association, Heinz Kohut, Otto F. Kernberg, or Christopher Lasch, Brick Pollitt displays many of the prominent features of the narcissistic personality. His unique position within the Pollitt family suggests that he also assumes the most prominent role in *Cat on a Hot Tin Roof*, eliciting the attention of each of the other characters (and the audience), taking advantage of those closest to him, and defining each of the other major players in relation to himself. Suffering from a narcissistic injury to his fundamental self, Brick takes out his revenge on everyone: he rejects Maggie's love and refuses to sleep with her; he informs Big Daddy of his impending death; as soon as Skipper fails to conform to Brick's ideal of friendship, Brick devalues and dismisses him. Significantly, Brick's narcissism helps to explain each of these relationships, just as it also helps to illuminate the relationship that Williams imagined between the playwright and his audience.

For Williams, Narcissus also represents the artist, who must, necessarily, seek the attention of an audience. In the prefatory remarks that introduce *Cat on a Hot Tin Roof*, Williams relates the following "parable," which suggests that the artist's role is both "a demand for attention" and a challenge to "ris[e] above the singular to the plural concern":

> I once saw a group of little girls on a Mississippi sidewalk, all dolled up in their mothers' and sisters' castoff finery, old raggedy ball gowns and plumed hats and high-heeled slippers, enacting a meeting of ladies in a parlor with a perfect mimicry of polite Southern gush and simper. But one child was not satisfied with the attention paid her enraptured performance by the others, they were too involved in their own performances to suit her, so she stretched out her skinny arms and threw back her skinny neck and shrieked to the deaf heavens and her equally oblivious playmates. "Look at me, look at me, look at me!"

Although silent throughout much of the play, Brick nevertheless speaks for the artist in Williams, his actions giving voice to the unarticulated cry, "Look at me, look at me, look at me!" His silence and his symptoms speak the "narcissistic discourse" that Lacan suggests the analyst must penetrate "in order to find in it what the subject is not saying." Both Brick and *Cat on a Hot Tin Roof* suggest that experience is not merely singular and personal but also public and plural. The suggested likeness between Narcissus and Brick not only emphasizes Brick's central role in *Cat on a Hot Tin Roof* (he is, after all, the one major character who appears on stage for a significant time during each of the three acts), but also raises Brick's personal malady to the level of a public concern. Brick's narcissism is meant to reflect American culture's self-interested focus and its unconscionable neglect of human needs. Part of Maggie's final speech to Brick—"What you want is someone to—[. . .]—take hold of you.—Gently, gently, with love!" (stage direction omitted)—is a recognition of Brick's tragic alienation and his unspoken desire "for a sense of connection with others." Echoing the voice of Maggie, and with the aid of myth, Williams speaks not only to the possible reformation of Brick but to that of society as well.

Chronology

1911   Thomas Lanier ("Tennessee") Williams born on March 26 in Columbus, Mississippi, to Cornelius Coffin and Edwina Dakin, a year-and-a-half after Tennessee's sister, Rose Isabel, is born.

1918   Family moves to St. Louis, Missouri, in July.

1919   Brother, Walter Dakin, is born.

1929   Graduates from University City High School, St. Louis. Enrolls in the University of Missouri in September.

1931–35   Works intermittently for International Shoe Company in St. Louis.

1935   Nervous breakdown. *Cairo, Shanghai, Bombay* is produced.

1936   Enrolls at Washington University in St. Louis.

1937   Enrolls at the University of Iowa.

1938   Graduates from the University of Iowa with a B.A. in English. Moves to Chicago, then New Orleans.

1939   Moves to New York.

1940   *Battle of Angels* produced. Works at odd jobs and as itinerant
         writer in various cities through 1944.

1943   Works as screenwriter at MGM. *You Touched Me* produced.

1944   *The Glass Menagerie* produced.

1945   *Stairs to the Roof* produced.

1947   Meets Frank Merlo, who becomes his long-time companion.
         Summer and Smoke and *A Streetcar Named Desire* produced.

1948   Awarded the Pulitzer Prize for *A Streetcar Named Desire*. *One
         Arm*, a collection of stories, published.

1950   *The Roman Spring of Mrs. Stone* published.

1951   *The Rose Tattoo* produced; receives Tony Award.

1952   Elected to lifetime membership in the National Institute of Arts
         and Letters.

1953   *Camino Real* produced.

1954   *Hard Candy*, a collection of stories, published.

1955   *Cat on a Hot Tin Roof* and *All in One*, featuring *Twenty-seven
         Wagons Full of Cotton*, are produced; awarded the Pulitzer Prize
         for *Cat on a Hot Tin Roof*.

1956   *In the Winter of Cities*, poetry, published; film, *Baby Doll*,
         released and nominated for Academy Award.

1957   *Orpheus Descending* produced. Father dies.

1958   *Garden District* (*Suddenly Last Summer* and *Something Unspoken*)
         produced.

1959   *Sweet Bird of Youth*; *I Rise in Flame, Cried the Phoenix*; and
         The Purification are produced.

1960   *Period of Adjustment* produced.

1961   *The Night of the Iguana* produced; film, *The Fugitive Kind*, released.

1962   Awarded a lifetime fellowship by the American Academy of Arts and Letters.

1963   *The Milk Train Doesn't Stop Here Anymore* produced. Frank Merlo dies.

1966   *Slapstick Tragedy* produced; book of stories, *The Knightly Quest*, is published.

1967   *The Two-Character Play* produced.

1968   *The Seven Descents of Myrtle* produced; *Kingdom of Earth* produced.

1969   *In the Bar of a Tokyo Hotel* produced; film, *Last of the Mobile Hot-Shots*, released.

1971   *Out Cry* produced.

1972   *Small Craft Warnings* produced.

1974   *Eight Mortal Ladies Possessed*, a collection of short stories, published.

1975   *The Red Devil Battery Sign* produced. *Moise and the World of Reason* and *Memoirs* published.

1976   *Letters to Donald Windham* published; and *This Is (An Entertainment)* produced.

1977   *Vieux Carré* produced. *Androgyne, Mon Amour*, a book of poems, is published.

1978   *Where I Live* published.

1979   *A Lovely Sunday for Creve Coeur* and *Kirche, Kutchen und Kinder* produced. First issue of the *Tennessee Williams Newsletter* is published.

1980   *Clothes for a Summer Hotel* produced. Mother dies. Awarded Presidential Medal of Freedom.

1981   *Something Cloudy, Something Clear* and *A House Not Meant to Stand* produced.

1983   Dies night of February 24–25 at the Hotel Elysée in New York City. Last issue of the *Tennessee Williams Review*.

1985   *Collected Stories* are published.

1989   First issue of the *Tennessee Williams Literary Journal* is published.

Contributors

HAROLD BLOOM is Sterling Professor of the Humanities at Yale University and Henry W. and Albert A. Berg Professor of English at the New York University Graduate School. He is the author of over 20 books, including *Shelley's Mythmaking* (1959), *The Visionary Company* (1961), *Blake's Apocalypse* (1963), *Yeats* (1970), *A Map of Misreading* (1975), *Kabbalah and Criticism* (1975), *Agon: Toward a Theory of Revisionism* (1982), *The American Religion* (1992), *The Western Canon* (1994), and *Omens of Millennium: The Gnosis of Angels, Dreams, and Resurrection* (1996). *The Anxiety of Influence* (1973) sets forth Professor Bloom's provocative theory of the literary relationships between the great writers and their predecessors. His most recent books include *Shakespeare: The Invention of the Human*, a 1998 National Book Award finalist, and *How to Read and Why*, which was published in 2000. In 1999, Professor Bloom received the prestigious American Academy of Arts and Letters Gold Medal for Criticism.

ROGER BOXILL has been a professor of English at the City College of the City University of New York. He is the author of *Shaw and the Doctors* and has been the New York theater correspondent for the *Shakespeare Quarterly*.

JOHN M. CLUM teaches drama and speech at Duke University. He is an author and editor.

GEORGE W. CRANDELL teaches English at Auburn University. He is the author of *The Critical Response to Tennessee Williams*, as well as a bibliography on Ogden Nash.

ALICE GRIFFIN has been a theater editor, critic, and a university teacher. She is the author of a number of literary criticism titles.

SUSAN KOPRINCE teaches English at the University of North Dakota.

CHARLES E. MAY is a professor of English at California State University at Long Beach. He is the editor and author of a number of books, including *Interacting with Essays* and works of literary criticism.

MARIAN PRICE has taught American literature at the Paedagogische Hochschule in Germany.

DAVID SAVRAN teaches English at Brown University. He is the author of books on theater and culture, including *Communists, Cowboys, & Queers: The Politics of Masculinity in the Work of Arthur Miller & Tennessee Williams*. He also has directed numerous plays and operas.

CHRISTOPHER BRIAN WEIMER teaches in the foreign language department at Oklahoma State University. Along with Barbara Simerka he has written the book *Echoes & Inscriptions: Comparative Approaches to Early Modern Spanish Literature*.

MARK ROYDEN WINCHELL teaches English at Clemson University. He is the author of numerous works of literary criticism.

Bibliography

Adler, Thomas P. "Culture, Power, and the (En)gendering of Community: Tennessee Williams and Politics," *Mississippi Quarterly* 48, no. 4 (Fall 1995): pp. 649–65.

Allen, Dennis W. "Homosexuality and Artifice in *Cat on a Hot Tin Roof*," *Coup de Théâtre* 5 (December 1985): pp. 71–78.

Barrick, Mac E. "Maggie the Cat: Tennessee Williams' Yerma." In *American Notes and Queries: Supplement I: Studies in English and American Literature*. Troy, N.Y.: Whitston, 1979.

Blackwell, Louise. "Tennessee Williams and the Predicament of Women." In *Critical Essays on Tennessee Williams*, ed. Robert A. Martin. New York: G. K. Hall, 1977, pp. 243–48.

Carpenter, Charles A. "Studies of Tennessee Williams' Drama: A Selective International Bibliography: 1966–1978," *Tennessee Williams Newsletter* 2 (Spring 1980): pp. 11–23.

Crandell, George W. *Tennessee Williams: A Descriptive Bibliography*. Pittsburgh: University of Pittsburgh, 1995.

Ganz, Arthur. "The Desperate Morality of the Plays of Tennessee Williams," *American Scholar* 31 (Spring 1962): pp. 278–94.

Gates, Jonathan. "Williams's Language of the Soul in *Glass Menagerie, Streetcar Named Desire*, and *Cat on a Hot Tin Roof*." In *Proceedings: Northeast Regional Meeting of the Conference on Christianity and Literature*, ed. Joan F. Hallisey and Mary Anne Vetterling. Weston, Mass.: Regis College, 1996.

Hale, Allean. "How a Tiger Became the Cat," *Tennessee Williams Literary Journal* 2, no. 1 (Winter 1990–91): pp. 33–36.

Hirsch, Foster. *A Portrait of the Artist: The Plays of Tennessee Williams*. Port Washington, N.Y.: Kennikat Press, 1980.

Hurd, Myles Raymond. "Cats and Catamites: Achilles, Patroclus, and Williams' *Cat on a Hot Tin Roof*," *Notes on Mississippi Writers* 23, no. 2 (June 1991): pp. 63–66.

Inge, M. Thomas. "The South, Tragedy, and Comedy in Tennessee Williams's *Cat on a Hot Tin Roof*." In *The United States South: Regionalism and Identity*, ed. Valeria Lerda, Tjebbe Westendorp, and Geo Pistarino. Rome: Bulzoni, 1991, pp. 157–65.

Isaac, Dan. "Big Daddy's Dramatic Word Strings," *American Speech* 40 (December 1965): pp. 272–78.

Jones, Robert Emmet. "Tennessee Williams' Early Heroines," *Modern Drama* 2 (December 1959): pp. 211–19.

Kalson, Albert E. "A Source for *Cat on a Hot Tin Roof*," *Tennessee Williams Newsletter* 2, no. 2 (Fall 1980): pp. 21–22.

Kataria, Gulshan Rai. "Animal Images in Tennessee Williams," *Indian Journal of American Studies* 21, no. 2 (Summer 1991): pp. 79–86.

———. *The Faces of Eve: A Study of Tennessee Williams's Heroines.* New Delhi: Sterlin, 1992.

———. "A Hetaira of Tennessee Williams: Maggie," *Indian Journal of American Studies* 12, no. 1 (1982): pp. 45–55.

Kolin, Philip C. "Tennessee in the '90s: Recent Scholarship on Tennessee Williams," *Publications of the Mississippi Philological Association* (1997): pp. 1–6.

Kullman, Colby H. "Rule by Power: 'Big Daddyism' in the World of Tennessee Williams's Plays," *Mississippi Quarterly* 48, no. 4 (Fall 1995): pp. 667–76.

Leverich, Lyle. *Tom: The Unknown Tennessee Williams.* New York: Crown, 1995.

Lilly, Mark. "Tennessee Williams." In *American Drama*, ed. Clive Bloom. New York: St. Martin's Press, 1995, pp. 70–81.

Lux, Mary F. "Tennessee among the Lotus-Eaters: Drugs in the Life and Fiction of Tennessee Williams," *Southern Quarterly* 38, no. 1 (Fall 1999): pp. 117–23.

Martin, Robert A., ed. *Critical Essays on Tennessee Williams.* New York: G. K. Hall, 1997.

Mayberry, Susan Neal. "A Study of Illusion and the Grotesque in Tennessee Williams' *Cat on a Hot Tin Roof*," *Southern Studies* 22 (1983): pp. 359–65.

Morrow, Laura and Edward Morrow. "Can *Cat on a Hot Tin Roof* Reach Equilibrium? Multicriticism, the Gaia Theory, and Tennessee Williams," *Synthesis* 1, no. 1 (Spring 1995): pp. 19–40.

Murphy, Brenda. "Brick Pollitt Agonistes: The Game in 'Three Players of a Summer Game' and *Cat on a Hot Tin Roof*," *Southern Quarterly* 38, no. 1 (Fall 1999): pp. 36–44.

O'Connor, Jacqueline. *Dramatizing Dementia: Madness in the Plays of Tennessee Williams.* Bowling Green, Ohio: Popular, 1997.

Parker, Brian. "A Preliminary Stemma for Drafts and Revisions of Tennessee Williams' *Cat on a Hot Tin Roof* (1955)," *Papers of the Bibliographical Society of Canada* 90, no. 4 (December 1996): pp. 475–96.

Ramaswamy, S. "Geriatrics: The Treatment of Old Age in Tennessee Williams's Plays," *Indian Journal of American Studies* 28, nos. 1–2 (Winter–Summer 1998): pp. 1–6.

Roudané, Matthew C., ed. *The Cambridge Companion to Tennessee Williams.* Cambridge: Cambridge University Press, 1997.

Sahu, Dharanidhar. *Cats on a Hot Tin Roof: A Study of Alienated Characters in the Major Plays of Tennessee Williams.* Delhi: Academic Foundation, 1990.

Saksteder, William. "*The Three Cats:* A Study in Dramatic Structure," *Drama Survey* 5 (Winter 1966–67): pp. 252–66.

Sarotte, Georges Michel. "Fluidity and Differentiation in Three Plays by Tennessee Williams: *The Glass Menagerie, A Streetcar Named Desire*, and *Cat on a Hot Tin Roof*." In *Staging Difference: Cultural Pluralism in American Theatre and Drama*, ed. Marc Maufort. New York: Peter Lang, 1995.

Savran, David. *Communists, Cowboys, and Queers: The Politics of Masculinity in the Works of Arthur Miller and Tennessee Williams.* Minneapolis: University of Minnesota Press, 1992.

Shackelford, Dean. "The Truth That Must Be Told: Gay Subjectivity, Homophobia, and Social History in *Cat on a Hot Tin Roof*," *Tennessee Williams Annual Review* 1 (1998): pp. 103–18.

Tharpe, Jac, ed. *Tennessee Williams: 13 Essays*. Jackson: University Press of Mississippi, 1980.

Timpane, John. "'Weak and Divided People': Tennessee Williams and the Written Woman." In *Feminist Rereadings of Modern American Drama*, ed. June Schlueter. Rutherford, N.J.: Fairleigh Dickinson University Press, 1989, pp. 171–80.

Tischler, Nancy M. "On Creating Cat," *Tennessee Williams Literary Journal* 2, no. 2 (1991–92): pp. 9–16.

Wolter, Jürgen C. "Strangers on Williams' Stage," *Mississippi Quarterly* 49, no. 1(Winter 1995–96): pp. 33–52.

Acknowledgments

"Brick Pollitt as Homo Ludens: 'Three Players of a Summer Game' and *Cat on a Hot Tin Roof*," by Charles E. May. From *Tennessee Williams: 13 Essays*, Jac Tharpe, ed. © 1980 by the University Press of Mississippi. Reprinted by permission.

"*Cat on a Hot Tin Roof*," by Roger Boxill. From *Tennessee Williams*. © 1987 by Roger Boxill. Reprinted by permission of Palgrave Publishers Ltd.

"'Something Cloudy, Something Clear': Homophobic Discourse in Tennessee Williams," by John M. Clum. From *The South Atlantic Quarterly* 88, no. 1 (Winter 1989). © 1989 by Duke University Press. Reprinted by permission.

"'By Coming Suddenly into a Room That I Thought Was Empty': Mapping the Closet with Tennessee Williams," by David Savran. From *Studies in the Literary Imagination* 24, no. 2 (Fall 1991). © 1991 by the Department of English, Georgia State University. Reprinted by permission.

"Journeys from Frustration to Empowerment: *Cat on a Hot Tin Roof* and Its Debt to García Lorca's *Yerma*," by Christopher Brian Weimer. From *Modern Drama* 35, no. 4 (December 1992). © 1992 by the University of Toronto. Reprinted by permission.

"Tennessee Williams's Unseen Characters," by Susan Koprince. From *The Southern Quarterly* 33, no. 1 (Fall 1994). © 1994 by the University of Southern Mississippi. Reprinted by permission.

"Come Back to the Locker Room Ag'in, Brick Honey!" by Mark Royden Winchell. From *The Mississippi Quarterly* 48, no. 4 (Fall 1995). © 1995 by Mississippi State University. Reprinted by permission.

"*Cat on a Hot Tin Roof:* The Uneasy Marriage of Success and Idealism," by Marian Price. From *Modern Drama* 38, no. 3 (Fall 1995). © 1995 by the University of Toronto. Reprinted by permission.

"*Cat on a Hot Tin Roof,*" by Alice Griffin. From *Understanding Tennessee Williams.* © 1995 by the University of South Carolina. Reprinted by permission.

"'Echo Spring': Reflecting the Gaze of Narcissus in Tennessee Williams's *Cat on a Hot Tin Roof,*" by George W. Crandell. From *Modern Drama* 42, no. 3 (Fall 1999). © 1999 by the University of Toronto. Reprinted by permission.

Index